Citizens an

Citizens and Exiles

CHRISTIAN FAITH
IN A PLURAL WORLD

*

Michael Nazir-Ali

First published in Great Britain in 1998 by
SPCK, Marylebone Road, London NW1 4DU

The Scripture quotations in this book are from the
Revised Standard Version of the Bible © 1971 and 1952

The version of the Qu'rān used is that of A. Yusuf 'Ali,
The Holy Qu'rān: Text, Translation and Commentary
© Leicester, Islamic Foundation, 1975

British Library Cataloguing-in-Publication Data
A catalogue record for this book is available from the British Library

ISBN 0 281 05050 3

Typeset by Wilmaset Ltd, Birkenhead, Wirral
Printed in Great Britain by
Arrowsmiths, Bristol

Contents

For Shammy and Ross,
in whose world Christ is being rediscovered.

Preface

This book is the fruit of numerous conversations with Christians and other people of faith, as well as with those of no declared faith. They have taken place in every part of the world and in the most diverse circumstances imaginable.

Both in my work in preparation for the 1998 Lambeth Conference and as General Secretary of the Church Mission Society, I have had the immense privilege of getting to know the very different contexts in which Christians bear witness to their faith today. I am very grateful indeed to all of those who have shared their joys and sorrows with me. Needless to say, while the riches are theirs, the opinions (and errors) are mine!

These days it is very difficult for diocesan bishops to find time for writing. That this book has been written at all is due to the able assistance of my Chaplain, the Revd Paul Williams, and my Private Secretary, Miss Gillian Keating. I owe a great debt of gratitude to them and to my Editor at SPCK, Linda Hurcombe.

Michael Nazir-Ali
Feast of St Peter and St Paul, 1998

PART ONE

*What Christians Believe
about God*

1

Religious Faith in a Changing World

*

I dreamt I dwelt in marble halls . . .
And woke to find it true,
I wasn't born for an age like this
Was Smith, was Jones, were you?
(Alfred Bunn)[1]

We live in a highly mobile age. The rate of change in the speed of travel, for instance, is exponential; in just over half a day, you can be at the other side of the world! There is also a continuing explosion in information, technology and communications. A fax from the other side of the world can be on your desk within a few minutes of having been sent, and information from the world's markets can be flashed onto your screens instantaneously.

Because of this mobility, and also because of disturbances such as civil war and terrorism, people of many different kinds now live 'cheek by jowl' with each other. The movement of peoples is one of the great 'givens' of our times. This is *not* to be understood simply as the movement of 'economic' migrants and refugees from Africa, Asia and Latin America to the West. Previous generations of refugees fled from religious and political persecution in Europe to, say, the Americas. Subsequent colonial enterprise settled hundreds of millions of Europeans in the Americas, in Australasia, in Africa and in Asia. The most substantial movements of people take place, of course, within continents and even within particular countries.

One of the results of these mass movements has been that people of different beliefs, values and cultures have become neighbours

3

and have, therefore, become aware of each other's way of life and world view. Such awareness does not, of course, depend on geographical proximity. We can develop this sort of awareness through travel and even through the mass media.

In certain societies, this awareness of plurality can create or widen the possibilities of choice. In many societies, there have always been some possibilities of choice within or between religious traditions. Now these have been greatly extended to include even the most exotic options. Totalitarian systems, whether of family, religion or nation, can keep these choices at bay for a while. But the sheer mobility of today's world works against them, and their citadels are daily challenged and eroded.

In situations where personal liberty and communal freedom are valued, we find that people do exercise the choice available to them. A certain amount of individual autonomy and social privacy makes it possible for subcultures to emerge. These are usually grouped around common beliefs and values. Many contemporary societies now consist of these clusters of subcultures and have to be understood in this way.

The reality of our plural world and the ubiquity of choice were driven home to me recently when I was doing a series of programmes for the BBC. The programme consisted of a panel discussing various questions of beliefs and values in the world today. My colleagues on the panel were a Hindu, a Buddhist, a Jew and a Muslim. 'What is so remarkable about that?' you may ask. Well, you see, the Hindu was a true Cockney, the Buddhist was a lady of middle years from the Home Counties and the Jew was a woman Rabbi! I was, of course, the Christian representative and only the Muslim seemed 'typical' in terms of origin and language. Not only had 'choices' been made, all of us also belonged to groups where others too had made a choice.

Plural Does Not Mean Pluralistic

Such a plural situation can lead people to take a view that is *pluralistic*; where different beliefs and values are regarded as, more or less, equally valid and none of them is seen as especially privileged. It is important to note the difference between 'plural' and 'pluralistic' at the outset. The term 'plural' is simply about the way things are in a given society. 'Pluralistic', however, has to do with an ideological, even theological, estimate of such a situation and its implications for society at large. In many areas of policy, education, for example, approaches have been informed by an implicit pluralism which has only recently begun to be challenged. It is also often the case that 'pluralistic' attitudes, while paying lip-service to the equal validity of different systems of belief, actually marginalize all of them. Bishop Lesslie Newbigin has pointed out over many years and in several books how pluralism consigns belief, world views and values to a private sphere from where they are not permitted to influence public policy.[2]

As we embark on an examination of Christian beliefs and attitudes in the contemporary world, we are conscious that we must carry out our task in a plural context. Christian faith has not only to be expressed in terms which are intelligible for those of other faiths and of no faith, it has also to relate to the concerns of these groups. How it relates will vary from faith to faith and from issue to issue. Sometimes there will be an acknowledgement of complementarity, at others, there may be challenge, and at yet others, categories of fulfilment and recapitulation may need to be employed.

There is, of course, another approach. This sees Christianity as an apprehension and articulation of the ultimately 'Real' in particular cultural and historical terms. Other faiths and, by extension, other ways of life apprehend and articulate the ultimately 'Real' in ways related to their own cultural and historical circumstances. All are equally valid in their own terms and we should see these different 'ways of life' as illuminating particular aspects of the 'Real'. The name most associated with this approach is, of course, that of John Hick. It is well-known that Hick has suggested a 'Copernican' revolution in the study of religions so that other religions are not studied from the dogmatic standpoint of one's own. Rather, God is seen at the centre and all religions are seen as serving him and revolving around him.[3] While differences among religions are not to be ignored, they are best accounted for in terms of particular histories and cultural developments. Hick's view has been trenchantly criticised by Gavin D'Costa who points out that the God put at the centre by Hick is the Judaeo-Christian God who has been illegitimately smuggled back into the discussion! Hick's axiom of God's universal love and desire to serve all people, he has learnt from Christianity.

According to D'Costa, such a pluralist position is flawed because it assumes something to be true, while denying the validity and normative status of those events that reveal and are part of the truth.[4] To this we may add that, if such as the case, then it also fails to treat other faiths with the integrity they deserve. It does not deal fully with what is ultimately significant for these other faiths and does not satisfactorily examine the compatibility of its own axioms of Christian origin with the basic beliefs of followers of other faiths.

Hick's 'Copernican' revolution was, of course, not as new as it seemed. In important respects, he had been anticipated by the distinguished Indian philosopher and President, Sarvepalli Radhakrishnan. Radhakrishnan was inspired by the non-dualist, idealistic nature of classical Hinduism. This led him to emphasize the unity of the world and of humankind. The different religions were seen as culturally and historically determined 'forms' of universal truth and needed to be shown their essential oneness. Radhakrishnan's thought was, of course, to be understood in the context of the communal traumas leading up to, and following, Indian independence. It has also to be recognized that it has found considerable sympathy among Western intellectuals influenced by the *philosophia perennis* tradition which teaches that the apprehension of reality is possible in all cultures and religions by considering the natural order and human values.[5] It can be said, however, that Radhakrishnan's position is open to the same criticism as Hick's: the categories of *advaita*, or non-dualistic Hinduism, are regarded as basic, and other religions are interpreted in their light. The historical and theological particularity on which Judaism, Christianity and Islam insist is neglected in favour of trying to discern 'universal truth' in all the religions.

If we cannot take this 'indifferentist' approach to the various religions, nor can we adopt the extreme 'neo-orthodox' position typified in the early work of Hendrik Kraemer. Kraemer has emphasized the principle of discontinuity. Non-Christian religions are simply the result of human effort and are inevitably affected by human sinfulness. There can be no point of contact between them and the gospel of God's unique self-disclosure in Jesus Christ, even in terms of the latter fulfilling the former. It needs to be pointed out that for Kraemer and his followers, Christianity, in its cultic, literary and even theological forms is a religion like the other religions in that it stands under the judgement of the gospel, even if the gospel is known through the historical forms of Christian tradition. Later on, Kraemer modified his position somewhat and was more willing to acknowledge some sort of 'general revelation' in non-Christian religions. Even so, the response to this is mixed and is affected by human sinfulness. The other faiths may show us some of our need of God but are not adequate in meeting this need. The Gospel alone reveals fully the extent of our need and how we must accept by grace and through faith God's gracious provision for this need in the life, death and resurrection of Jesus Christ.[6]

The Study of Religion: Professional or Confessional?

In trying to make sense of the plurality all around us, we need to be on guard against two opposite dangers. One is the view that we can somehow be objective in our study of the various world views and values we encounter. This is an assumption that is sometimes made in the academic study of religions. The scholar is seen as a somewhat neutral observer who can describe, test and evaluate the different religious systems in a scientific way without bias towards any of them. The disciplines of the phenomenology of religion and of the history of religions have sometimes been affected by such an approach.

The other view is that religions can only be studied from a 'committed' point of view. All theology is confessional and we can make sense of our plural world only through the perspective of our credal commitments. We cannot, even if we wished to do so, transcend the boundaries set by our own tradition.

We are, however, coming to realize that it is not necessary to polarize the situation in this way. It is true that no one can be truly 'neutral' in this area of study. We all bring our presuppositions, perhaps even our commitments, to the study of our plural world or some specific aspect of it. If this is so in the fields of the physical and life sciences, how much more in the social sciences and particularly in the field of religion? Academic integrity demands that we should not ignore such a state of affairs but, rather, should acknowledge and take account of it. Such an acknowledgement should not paralyse academic endeavour in this area. There is a proper place for the academic study of religions, world views and values. Beliefs and practices need to be observed, classified and explained. Texts have to be examined critically so that reliable ones may be established. Histories of particular systems need to be written, revised and written again. Beliefs have to be described and tested for coherence and correspondence in the context of wider, perhaps even universal, systems of discourse. Bishop Kenneth Cragg has written of the 'accountability' of the world's religions, both to each other and in the wider world.[7] Disciplines which encourage such accountability should be found in faculties of theology and religious studies.

Universities, in particular, need to be places where people from different confessional backgrounds can meet, discover common interests and be challenged by the differences among them. This is not to deny that confessional estimates of world religions and ideologies can take place in university settings. It is entirely proper for them to do so both in universities and in confessional institutions such as theological colleges and study centres. It is important, however, that such confessional study should not be fideistic. That is to say, it must not imagine that its beliefs and values are true simply because they are the beliefs and values of the tradition to which the student belongs. Religious and ideological systems certainly have their own distinctive place but they should also be open to others for testing, evaluation and even, perhaps, reception.

The so-called 'Yale' theologians have pointed out that faith is passed on in the narrative traditions of a community and cannot be understood apart from them. For many years Lesslie Newbigin has been saying much the same thing about the passing on of all knowledge, scientific, literary or religious. Knowledge is acquired and transmitted within specific social and intellectual traditions. It is not possible, in such a context, to be neutral. One must belong to a 'tradition of rationality'. Both Newbigin and the 'Yale' theologians are concerned, however, not to neglect the mission dimension: how is the Christian faith, which is expressed in a particular kind of language and which is transmitted within specific cultural frameworks, to be communicated to those outside the tradition? Is it merely a matter of people discerning the lineaments of the biblical narrative in the love and life of the Christian community, or are interpretative skills also needed? If they are, what is the extent to which the Church can engage with the cultural values and world views around it?[8]

If it is true that knowledge, including religious knowledge, is passed on within social and cultural traditions, it is also true that these traditions are subject to significant, even radical, change. Such change may occur from the force of external pressures such as prosperity or poverty, technological development or social change. It can also occur from within because some principle of self-criticism, embedded in the tradition, comes to the fore. Such a principle is at work, for example, in the prophetic critique in the Hebrew Bible of cult, kingship and even law. This critique changed the fundamental orientation of Hebrew religion away from concepts of holiness rooted in cultic practices towards a more ethically based view of righteousness.[9] It was continued in the life and ministry of Jesus, particularly in his emphasis on inward transformation as a basis for a right relationship with God and with our neighbours. Such a view of the human condition and what needs to be done about it is very far indeed from the cultic sacrifices of animals and of agricultural produce – as a way of access to God.

In an important passage, Newbigin compares the world view of Saivite poets writing in Tamil with the world view of an English Christian missionary (himself). He concludes that the two can be made intelligible to each other in only a very limited way and that the real question is about choice: which world view is more adequate for grasping and coping with reality?[10] Many would see in this question, posed in so sharp a form, the religious equivalent of Macaulay's educational policy in India which preferred one book from the libraries of Europe over all the wisdom, philosophy and spirituality of the East! More importantly, perhaps, we have to ask whether intelligibility is as limited as Newbigin makes out and whether choosing between one or other view is the only option left to us.

The Transformation of Traditions

Is it possible to say that a tradition may be modified, or even changed radically, because of an encounter with another tradition? The history of Christian mission gives us a clue. As the faith spread outwards from its Judaic background, it had to be expressed in the spiritual terminology of the people it encountered. The form in which the New Testament writings have come down to us itself bears witness to this. It is not only that the language used is Koine

Greek but there is a profound engagement with Gentile cultures which the Church first encountered. This is shown not only in the use of religious terms and concepts but also, for instance, in an awareness of world views, ethical codes of behaviour and even popular religiosity.

By the time the New Testament came to be written, there was already a fairly developed form of apologetic in the Hellenistic-Jewish tradition. This apologetic was in the Jewish 'Wisdom' mould and was influential in the shaping of Christian apologetics from the New Testament period and onwards.

Justin Martyr and Clement of Alexandria were two early Christian apologists from the second century AD. In his *Dialogue with Trypho the Jew*, Justin bases his argument on the prophecies and teachings of the Hebrew Bible. In doing this, he is, of course, following a precedent already well-established in the New Testament. In their approach to the Gentiles, however, both apologists appeal, first of all, to Reason as the divine attribute by which all people have been enlightened. It is this which has enabled them to turn away from superstition and towards the truth. At this point, the apologists, relying heavily on the prologue to St John's Gospel, claim that this very Reason, Wisdom or God's Eternal Word (*Logos*) became incarnate in Jesus of Nazareth to reveal God's purposes fully and definitively so that there would be no excuse for people to remain in darkness and error. It is true that this revelation was despised and rejected by those who preferred to remain in their sinful ways, but God has vindicated it, and all lovers of truth and goodness can recognize the Logos in Jesus Christ.

The apologists saw the divine Reason, definitively revealed in Christ, also at work in the philosophy of the Gentile world. This was recognized, particularly, in the Stoic view that the universe must be seen as a balanced and harmonious whole ordered by Reason or the Logos. Clement adds that such a harmony is not already achieved. Indeed, it has been disrupted and needs to be restored. It is the Logos, revealed in Christ, who restores the universe to its intended harmony and who 'tunes' humanity in such a way that it is in harmony with the Holy Spirit.

Poetry, too, even though pre-occupied with falsehood, can still speak of God. Poets have received some of the 'sparks' of divine Reason and have voiced important aspects of the truth. Clement provides numerous quotations from the poets which confirm the preaching of the Gospel. There are resonances here with Paul at Athens and his appeal to the poets (Acts 17.22–31).

Already in the New Testament, in the 'household codes' of Ephesians and Colossians, for instance, there was a recognition that God was at work in the practical morality taught by groups such as the Stoics. These codes were adopted and adapted for Christian use – although, as C. F. D. Moule points out, the emphasis here is on the mutuality of relationships within a household. Such mutuality, apparently, not being prominent in the pagan world![11]

Surprisingly, perhaps, the apologists also allowed that Gentile prophecy could be a divinely inspired source of truth. Greek sibyls of various periods were specifically regarded as having prophesied the coming of Christ. The so-called Sibylline Oracles were extensively used by the Christian apologists of the second century, even though, by this time, the oracles had become subject to Jewish apocalyptic influence. The important point, however, for our purposes is that the apologists were not aware of this influence and evaluated these oracles as of purely Gentile origin.[12]

Such an engagement certainly facilitated the propagation of Christianity in the ancient world, but it also brought about a change, sometimes a significant change, in the traditions with which the engagement took place. Bishop Kenneth Cragg has pointed out that the whole character of Judaism, after the fall of Jerusalem in 70 AD, was affected by its engagement with emergent Christianity. He wants to hold this in balance with the recent, and justified, interest in the Jewish context of Jesus' ministry and the emergence of the Church.[13] In the same way, recent scholarship has shown that the shift in Neo-Platonism from being purely a philosophy to being a kind of mystery religion, occurred partly as a result of the encounter with Christianity. In fact, it can be said that Neo-Platonism, as a religion, was perhaps the most serious rival to Christianity in later antiquity.[14] Christianity's debt to Neo-Platonism is well-rehearsed. Here we see that there was a certain mutuality in the interaction.

Hinduism is known to have played a part in the development of Neo-Platonist philosophy, which was to influence Christian discourse so deeply; and also in the emergence of Neo-Platonism as a religious movement. In more recent times, however, the interaction has taken place in the context of the modern missionary movement. Christians have certainly learned and continue to learn from Hindus. This may be in forms of meditation or contemplation. It may be in terms of iconography or music. It may be in terms of a better understanding of the universe's harmony and unity. Hindu religious and social reformers, however, have also acknowledged a significant debt to Christianity where the religious, moral and social renewal of Hindu thought is concerned. This debt is evident in the emphasis on monotheism in much of Hinduism today, in attitudes towards caste and in the treatment of women.[15] The social action of Raja Ram Mohan Roy, the poetry of Rabindranath Tagore and the movement of *satyagraha*, or non-violent political action, initiated by Mahatma Gandhi were all acknowledged as being, at least in part, influenced and inspired by the Christian story.

As a movement, Sufism has produced much that is attractive in Islamic civilization. A great deal of the poetry, art and architecture of the Islamic world has been influenced by Sufi ideals. The roots of mysticism in Islam certainly go back to the Qu'rān and the Sunnah (or Practice) of the Prophet and his companions. Sufis have always, however, been glad to own the stimulus provided for their movement by the Christian monks and hermits of the Syrian and Egyptian deserts. Allama Muhammad Iqbal, the poet-philosopher of Pakistan, in a discussion on the origins of Sufism, identifies six conditions which gave rise to the movement. Prominent among them is 'the presence of Christianity as a working ideal of life'. Significantly, he goes on to say that it was the actual life of the Christian monks and hermits, rather than their religious ideas, which exercised such a fascination on the minds of the early Sufis.[16] Iqbal also refers to the persuasive influence of Persian categories of thought in the development of Sufism.

Bishop John V. Taylor, when he was still General Secretary of CMS, asked in a most pointed way about the transformation of religious traditions as they encounter one another. When we talk about mission, we often refer to the conversion of individuals or even of communities from one allegiance to another. For mission-ary faiths, such as Christianity and Islam, such talk is unavoidable. We also refer to the impact of local culture on a particular religious tradition and the tradition's influence on the culture. This too is necessary. It may be, however, that the most significant matter here is the transformation of a religious tradition as a result of an encounter with another tradition. In the past, ideas travelled slowly and influence was felt gradually. The pace of the interaction is much quicker now and, no doubt, the rate of change will be greater. It will be interesting to see whether and how religious traditions change as a result of encounter and interaction.

Intelligibility and Translatability

In my view, then, there is intelligibility and translatability between religious traditions so that at least some of the beliefs and values of the one can be explained to the other. This is the basis both of dialogue and of mutual accountability. I believe, moreover, that interaction between religious traditions results in change, not only for individual adherents, but often for the tradition as a whole. The study of any major world religion will show how traditions have changed because of influences from outside. At the same time we affirm that traditions are distinctive and, while they may learn from each other, they must not be confused with each other or forced into an artificial amalgam of one sort or another. Both 'distinctiveness' and a certain 'openness' are crucial to the task which follows.

> . . . And all is seared with trade; bleared, smeared with toil;
> And wears man's smudge and shares man's smell: . . .
> And for all this, nature is never spent;
> There lives the dearest freshness deep down things. . . .
> (G. M. Hopkins)[17]

2

A Sense of the Sacred

*

In her book *A History of God*, Karen Armstrong writes that her studies in the history of religion had shown her that human beings are spiritual animals. Religion was not born merely out of fear of powerful natural forces. Nor was it imposed on ordinary people by powerful alliances of priests and kings as a way of retaining and enhancing power. It was born, rather, as a way of expressing wonder and a sense of mystery about the world in which we live. In spite of the vicissitudes of nature and the fact of human suffering, religion is an attempt to find meaning and value in life.[1]

Until the emergence of the 'secularized' societies of the Western world, religion was universal and universally important. It is also, of course, breath-takingly diverse. Apart from the major world religions, there are numerous 'primal' or 'traditional' religions, some of them co-existing with a world faith. In addition, there are various cults which have arisen as a result of interaction between world faiths and primal world views.

Religions are often divided into the polytheistic, the mono-theistic and the idealistic (or absolutist). In some, a multiplicity of gods is positively celebrated, while others insist that a harmonious universe demands one creator – God, while yet others are of the view that such a harmony requires that, ultimately, the distinction between creator and creature should disappear. Another way of classifying religions is to distinguish between 'natural' and 'revealed' religion or between the 'cultic' and the 'prophetic'. It has to be said that these distinctions are sometimes quite arbitrary and there is considerable overlap between the different kinds of religion in real life. Nor do these categories exhaust every kind of religious expression. The Indic tradition alone yields several varieties of religion which are genuinely atheistic. Not only is atheism central to the Samkhya, Jain and Theravada Buddhist schools, much of their system has been elaborated to refute the arguments of the theists and idealists.

Given such diversity, is it possible to discern an underlying unity in the different expressions of the religious impulse? Whatever their distinctiveness, is there any area of common concern to all religions? Certain lines of enquiry may be possible. It seems to be the case that most religions are concerned with the 'Real' that underlies the flux of daily experience. This 'Real' is seen not only as the 'Ground of Being' but as the 'Transcendent' which provides order and meaning to the world in general and to human societies in particular.

In spite of the fact noted above that not all religions are theistic, it is a remarkable fact that for many there is a strong belief that at the basis of all created and manifested existence is an underlying, unifying reality which is the ultimate spiritual source of everything. Notwithstanding the metaphysics of religious systems, there is even a belief in a Supreme Being who is worshipped and honoured. Such a Being is often thought of in personal terms and is seen as endowed with love, intelligence and purpose.

A Supreme Being?

Anthropologists have for long been aware that behind the polytheistic multiplicity of primal or traditional religions, there is often a Supreme Being who may be neglected in practice but is seen as the source of a religion's spiritual heritage. In the African context, both John V. Taylor and Kwame Bediako from Ghana have pointed to the this-worldly character of African traditional religion. For Bediako, the spiritual and the physical are closely integrated in a unified cosmic system. The 'spiritual' aspects of such a system, moreover, have to do with a world of 'divinities, ubiquitous spirits, ancestors' and not only with a Supreme Being. There is not only constant intercourse between the mundane and the supra-mundane, there is a necessary continuity between the two realms. Bediako recognizes, nevertheless, the rightful place of the Supreme Being in such a system.[2]

John Mbiti, from the other side of Africa, has shown the universality of belief in a Supreme Being among African traditional religions. Given the great variety of cultures and contexts in which such religions have emerged and developed, this is, in itself, quite remarkable. Mbiti, however, goes on to show that many of the tribes, quite different now in language and culture, share the same name for God. He lists some of these common names for God: Chiuta, Jok, Leza, Mulungu, Nyame, Nzambi, etc. This suggests that belief in a Supreme Being is very ancient among the Bantu people of Africa, predating their migrations and the emergence of distinct cultures and languages.[3]

Because of the impact of Islam and Christianity, African writers have often emphasized the transcendent God of traditional religions, while playing down the significance of other aspects of African spirituality. Indeed, some of them, such as Bolaji Idowu of Nigeria, are prepared to see these aspects wither away as the flower of monotheism blooms.[4] As we might expect, others like Bediako are critical of such tendencies. They see both unity and multiplicity in the African world view. The Supreme Being is certainly a centre of spirituality and yet spiritual power is dispersed among ancestors and spirits. Such a distribution is, moreover, profoundly ambivalent. This ambivalence is seen clearly in the treatment given to the question of ancestors. Are ancestors worshipped or merely venerated? Is there a place for 'ancestor-reverence' in Christian worship? Such questions are not, of course, peculiar to the African situation. They have, in the past, arisen sharply in Asia. At the time of the emergence of the 'Chinese Rite', for example, Matteo Ricci, the famous Jesuit missionary, decided that the rituals in honour of the dead had only a civil significance and that Christians could engage in them without compromising their faith. It is true that, in the end, Rome ruled against Ricci and the Chinese Rite, but the problem remains a real one for many Chinese Christians today.[5]

For Bediako, a theology of ancestors becomes 'the corollary and unavoidable by-product of the continuity of God in African experience'. And yet it is clear that not all ancestors can be revered but only those who, in the words of Archbishop David Gitari of Kenya, 'were faithful to the Supreme God, before the arrival of the Gospel, as well as early converts'.[6] According to Mbiti, God himself is the Great Ancestor from whom all people, including human ancestors, and all things originated.[7] Bediako refers to Christ as 'Supreme Ancestor' because of his inclusive humanity to which human ancestors necessarily relate, and also because he is the source of all spiritual power and has triumphed over the 'principalities and powers' (Colossians 2.15).[8]

African writers may speculate about the origins of belief in a Supreme Being. They may claim that it arose from a primal reflection on nature or out of a sense of dependence or was, perhaps, suggested by powerful natural forces. In the end, however, they will often admit that they do not know too much about the origins of this belief, only that it can be shown to have existed from very ancient times.[9]

Is Monotheism Primal?

Turning from the Bantu peoples of Africa to the tribes of pre-Islamic Arabia, we find, once again, a Supreme Being who presides over a spiritual world consisting of lesser divinities, the jinn (or genii) and, of course, human beings themselves. Pre-Islamic Arabia is known by Muslims as the period of *Jahiliyya* (or ignorance). It was certainly a time of inter-tribal hostility and of fragmentation, even though the pilgrimage to the *Ka'aba* in Mecca provided a rallying point for some, at least, of the diverse Arab tribes. This was the situation that the Prophet of Islam, Muhammad, was called to purge and to reform. That, however, does not concern us now. The remarkable fact is that even at a time of such fragmentation, the tribes seem to have had a common belief in a high God whom they called Allah. The pre-Islamic history of this term is well-attested from both Arabic and non-Arabic sources, and the Qu'rān itself provides evidence of such usage.

Scholars have advanced different theories as to how the tribes came to have such a belief. One is the well-known 'amphictyony' theory. This became notorious when it was advanced by biblical scholars such as Albrecht Alt and Martin Noth to account for the emergence of ancient Israel. Alt and Noth held that the tribes had been bound together by the religious provisions of the Covenant, a common sanctuary at Shiloh and the synthesis of their various beliefs and histories into a common belief in Yahweh and a common patriarchal history. Alt and Noth's position has been criticized from various points of view, not least their failure to take sufficient account of the antiquity of certain provisions of the Covenant.[10] For our purposes, however, we need to note the well-established pattern of amphictyony-like alliances in the ancient world, whatever their religious content. With this in view, several authors have mooted the possibility that when the Arab tribes came together at the time of pilgrimage or for political and social reasons, the tribal god of each (*Al-ilah*) came to be regarded as the universal God (Allah). It is interesting, in this connection, that etymologically 'Allah' is related to '*ilah*'. Others have suggested that the term is borrowed from Syriac and is an arabicized form of the Christian *Alaha*. Nor can the influence of Judaism be discounted.[11]

But all of this assumes, as does the Graf-Wellhausen hypothesis in biblical studies, that monotheism is a developed and not a primal form of religion. It is held to emerge from polytheism, through henotheism (where only one god is worshipped, but the existence of others is not denied) and on to the strict worship of the one God as seen in the writing prophets of the Bible or in the Qu'rān. From the primal traditions, however, we learn that the names for the Supreme Being are of great antiquity, often of greater age than the names for lesser divinities, spirits and ancestors. Could it be that belief in a Supreme Being is actually the primal form of religion and that other aspects are elaborations and explanations? If such is the case, it may well be that the notion of a Supreme Being need not have been borrowed by the Arabs from elsewhere. Nor is it necessary that it should have evolved to legitimize political alliances. Whatever the terms used for such a Being, the concept and the experience could be native to the whole people and, indeed, to each tribe.

A Universal Sense of the Holy?

The Prince of Wales has repeatedly drawn attention to a near-universal 'sense of the sacred'.[12] In the most diverse traditions there is a sense of an underlying unity which is thought of as the ultimate source of all things. More than that, we have seen that sometimes, in spite of metaphysical systems, such a 'Ground of our being' is regarded both as infusing all things (immanent) and as being more than the sum of all things (transcendent). Such a Being is often conceived as personal, though it is also recognized that this category is not adequate and that such a Being should not be thought of as merely a person among others. The attributes of love, wisdom and purpose, with which such a Being is seen as endowed, however, cannot be thought of except in personal terms. Philosophical questions are sometimes raised about such a conception of God. It is asked, for instance, if every self has an 'other' over and against which it finds its identity, what would be an appropriate 'other' for an inclusive 'self' like God? Different traditions have posited nothingness, chaos or even creation (potential and actual) as an 'other' for God. The Christian doctrine of the Trinity sees the persons of the godhead as existing in a close relationship of love such that the identity of each can be described in terms of its relationship to the others.

Given an all-pervasive sense of the sacred and a widespread belief in a Supreme Being, how do these relate to the God of the Judaeo-Christian revelation? Are there any continuities to discern or must there be a sharp discontinuity? These are questions which have been asked whenever there has been a missionary encounter with the different human cultures and wherever 'the People of the Book' have encountered other religious traditions.

Revelation, Culture and Continuity

To some extent the answer depends on our view of revelation itself. If it is seen as something which descends from above, entirely *de novo*, and without the involvement of human faculties or of human culture, then, it is apparent that the discontinuities will be emphasized. This is indeed the case in varieties of fundamentalism in all the Abrahamic faiths. If, however, it is seen as an affirmation of much that is already believed, as well as a judgement on some customs and beliefs, then there can be a recognition of continuity. It cannot be denied that revelation brings something new to a situation, a context, a people, but such 'newness' often builds on the wisdoms and insights of the past. The newness consists in a brilliant synthesis, perhaps, of different aspects of the old not before related, or in a fresh interpretation of the old, or even in getting beyond the merely 'old' to the primal! Cragg, writing about the Jewishness of Jesus, points out that his significance lay not so much in the originality of his teaching but in what he calls Jesus' 'action in character': the clarity, courage and penetration with which he held his course and the inspiration he brought to those who heard him and the range of people he was able to address. To these we may add the freedom and freshness he brought to the interpretation of the Torah, the Writings and the Prophets.[13]

Revelation, moreover, is not only about the development and articulation, under God, of a people's experience, belief or custom. It can also be related to the assimilation and adaptation of stories, concepts and customs from outside. The Bible is full of rejection and judgement regarding some of the abominable practices of the people round about Israel (for example, the repeated condemnation of child-sacrifice). At the same time, however, there is a creative adaptation of stories, for instance, about creation. Even if scholars are now reluctant to speak of a direct 'borrowing' from Babylonian or Ras Shamra sources, it is clear that the creation stories in Genesis belong to a genre which had currency in the area. The stories have been adapted, however, precisely to make clear the theological purposes of the redactors. Instead of human beings being created as playthings or slaves of the gods, we find that they have been made in God's image and appointed his stewards.[14] Such assimilation and adaptation can also be shown, for example, in the treaty form of God's covenant with his people or in the building of the first Temple, or even in the writings of the poets and prophets of Israel.[15]

The Board of Mission study, *The Search for Faith*, points out that while certain practices of neighbouring peoples, such as human sacrifice, magic and divination are strictly rejected by the Hebrew Bible, others, having to do with the cult and many 'rites of passage' customs, are accepted and provided with new meanings. Similarly, in the Gospels, Jesus is shown as using popular customs like anointing with saliva (Mark 7.33; 8.23; cf. John 9.6–7), healing by touch (Luke 8.44), and by the laying on of hands (Luke 13.13). On the other hand, he condemns magical approaches to power and refuses to perform signs and wonders when they are understood in this way (Mark 8.11 and parallels).

In 1996 I was invited by the Archbishop of Central Africa to preach at the centenary celebrations for Bernard Mizeki's martyrdom. He was Zimbabwe's first Christian martyr and was murdered because he would not leave the people to whom he was a missionary at a time of great danger. I felt especially privileged to have been invited as the Diocese of Rochester is linked with the Diocese of Harare, where Mizeki's shrine is located. The celebrations were a most moving occasion, with people from many different parts of the world participating in different ways with music, dancing and prayer. As the preacher, naturally, I had tried to read what I could about Mizeki. I discovered that he had been determined from the outset to learn about the Mashona people to whom he had been sent by the Bishop. Not only had he learnt the language, Chishona, within a year of his arrival, he was also interested in learning about the spirituality of the people and their beliefs, particularly about the Great Spirit, *Mwari*. At the same time, he was not afraid to challenge superstition in the name of the Gospel.[16] It was very moving and illuminating, therefore, to discover the Church's Liturgy using the term 'Mwari' of God quite un-selfconsciously!

Bediako has reminded us that African Christian theology has generally been alert to the continuity between traditional religions and the Christian faith. This is seen particularly clearly in the continuity regarding belief in God: '. . . in virtually every Christian community in Africa, the Christian name for God is usually a divine name hallowed in the pre-Christian religious tradition for the Supreme God.'[17]

The Gospel: Transmission and Translatability

Such a situation can be paralleled in other contexts. Wherever the Scriptures have been translated, the traditional terms for God in a language or culture have been used, whether it is William Carey's choice of *Ishwar* for the Bible in Bengali or *Khuda* in Persian or, indeed, *Allah* in Arabic. In doing this, Bible translators, through the ages, have followed the example of the New Testament writings which use *Theos* for God. In the ancient world, this was a general name for 'divinity' and was not identified with any particular god, although it was used of each of the Greek pantheon.[18]

Nor need such a course of action be limited to terms for the divine being. Both testaments in the Bible are constantly using, adapting and stretching the meaning of terms taken from their immediate environment so that, somehow, the truth about God's dealings with creation may be communicated to people of specific cultures and languages. This process has continued in the life of the Church, as the Church has tried to adapt to the various peoples and cultures among whom it has found itself. The distinguished West

African theologian, now a professor at Yale, Lamin Sanneh, has drawn our attention to the 'translatability' of the Gospel. Included in this concept is the historical transmission of the Christian faith across cultures. Sanneh himself draws attention to the importance of Bible translation in this process. Unlike the scriptures of some other world faiths, the Bible can be effectively rendered into any human language without loss of its essential authenticity. But the really important truth about 'translatability' is not its transmission from cross-cultural missionary to indigenous communities; it is its assimilation within those communities. The translation of the Bible into indigenous languages and the assimilation of the Gospel into indigenous cultures speaks to Sanneh of God's preparatory work among these peoples and cultures so that they may be suitable receptacles for the Gospel message when it comes. He is clear that this includes, at least, aspects of traditional spirituality. Bediako has pointed out that such a view of translatability is profoundly incarnational. The Eternal Word incarnate in the culture and forms of first century Palestine, is seen as present in every culture and every place. In the process of historical transmission, 'the hidden reality of the divine presence' is brought to interact, indeed, brought to light, in the encounter with God's disclosure in Jesus Christ.'⁹

Fulfilment in Christ

African theologians such as Bediako, Mbiti and Sanneh are inching their way forward towards the development of what has been called a 'fulfilment' model of mission and culture. Such a model was also developed, for example, in the Christian encounter with Hinduism. This development goes much further back than most people imagine. It is still fashionable, for example, to castigate Victorian missionaries as benighted exclusivists who could see no good in the other faiths they encountered in Asia and Africa. Eric Sharpe has shown, however, that already in the nineteenth and earlier parts of the twentieth century, missionaries such as J. N. Farquhar and T. E. Slater were presenting Christianity not as hostile to other faiths, 'sounding the knell of doom' for them, but as a loyalty to One in whom Hindus (and others) would find realized and satisfied the noblest and earliest ideas of their own spiritual leaders and the deepest longings of their own hearts.

Alongside an impressive list of missionaries, Sharpe can also provide an equally important list of Indian Christians, such as K. M. Banerjea, Nehemiah Goreh and Brahmabandhav Upadyay, who also wished to see Christ as 'the recapitulation' of all that was best in Hinduism.

Sharpe points out that this movement did not end at the turn of the century but continued up to the outbreak of the Second World War in the work of Indians like A. J. Appasamy, Sundar Singh, P. Chenchaiah and V. Chakkarai. The impasse produced by the exclusivism of Hendrik Kraemer at the Tambaram Ecumenical Conference was also addressed by a distinguished company of Indian theologians in an influential symposium entitled *Rethinking Christianity in India*. 'A book,' remarks Sharpe, 'as far removed from monologue preaching as one could wish.'[20]

The period after the Second World War, Sharpe calls 'the great age of dialogue', and mentions, in particular, the important contribution made in this area by the Bangalore-based Christian Institute for the Study of Religion and Society (CISRS) and the work of its greatest theologians, Herbert Jai Singh and M. M. Thomas.

At its best, Hindu–Christian dialogue has been based on the deepest experience and longing for the divine on both sides. It has been based not just on a desire to know 'about' God but to 'know' God. That is, to experience the reality of God in the depths of the soul. It is this which has often driven Christians to seek the meaning of Hinduism in its contemplative tradition.[21]

The Question of God in Today's World

So far an impression may have been given that God or the Supreme Being or the Transcendent is simply a concern of the religions and of the religious, whether these are the great 'World Religions' or the more homely 'natural', 'folk' or 'traditional' religions of clans and tribes. Such is not the case, of course. God has always been of concern not only in philosophy and literature but also in the arts and sciences. There is currently a revival of interest in considering the question of God from these points of view and it will repay us to engage with at least some of them.

In what is widely regarded as a landmark work, George Steiner attempts to show that language about God is not just a relic of the past, like pre-Copernican expressions in our language about the sun 'rising' or 'setting'. It is not like a giant leviathan grounded on Dover Beach while the tide of faith has gone out. It is rather what gives the rest of language structure, meaning and purpose. It is what makes intellectual and aesthetic encounter possible, and it is what provides for the 'necessary possibility' of insight into transcendence which makes art and literature worthwhile. Steiner is aware that such views which see language as emblematic of order in the universe are under attack from those who would not only deny the Logos-inspired nature of the world and, therefore, of our language, but would deconstruct language in such a way that it no longer relates to what is, not even to 'I am'. Such a view of the world and of language has led to widespread nihilism and to the 'absence' of God in human discourse – and, yet, argues Steiner, the real question behind all literature and art remains: is there a God or not?

The 'presence' or 'absence' of God is, unavoidably, tied up with the question of meaning. The human quest, obstinately, remains theological. Steiner compares our times to the Saturday between Good Friday and Easter. It is a time of waiting, of questioning and of reflection. It *is* a time to think about the world's suffering and of its emptiness, but it is also a time of *hope*. Such 'sabbatarian waiting' however, needs to be informed by the rumour of God – and by language about God.[22]

The life and work of the novelist William Golding is an example of the perception that life is not only dreary and empty but also that there is downright wickedness and evil to be found in it. At the same time, Golding was acutely aware both of God's immanence in the human condition and even of the possibility of glimpsing transcendence through the darkness and sickness of the human mind. He believed that there was a profound mystery at the heart of the cosmos to which, nevertheless, human beings would be admitted. In spite of the undoubted bleakness of some of his work, such a vision was at the basis of the hope with which his work is shot through. Golding's realistic assessment of the human situation, along with his awareness of humanity's spiritual nature, is characteristic of great literature in any age and any culture. It is also, of course, consonant with a Christian anthropology derived from the Bible.[23]

The question about God is being asked not only in art and

literature; in the sciences too a debate is raging. In the last century there was a tendency among some scientists to treat physics as a paradigm for all sciences. In principle, everything could be reduced to the principles of Newtonian physics which were, themselves, fixed and unalterable. Such a mechanistic view of the world had no room for a God who was active in history. The most that could be allowed was a deistic 'First Mover' and even that became unnecessary if the universe was thought of as eternal with cause and effect going back in an infinite (but not vicious) regress.

The emergence of Quantum theory and then Quantum mechanics among scientists studying the smallest components of nature has introduced the possibility of indeterminism in even the physical world. This has challenged, in a radical way, mechanistic views of the world and has enabled scientists to ask questions about the nature of the universe in ways which sometimes resonate with Christian concerns.

Interest in the question of God from physical scientists, such as astronomers and cosmologists, however, has begun to arise from observations of the *systemic* aspects of the universe and the need to account for the stability of such systems. There are two interrelated aspects of this interest which are, perhaps, worth noting. One has to do with a fascination for the 'fine-tuning' which scientists find in the universe. Paul Davies observes that, 'a universe as smooth as ours requires some extraordinarily delicate fine-tuning at the outset, so that all regions of the universe expand in a carefully orchestrated manner.'[24] Bishop Hugh Montefiore, although not a scientist himself, considers not only the fine-tuning in the universe in terms, for example, of its rate of expansion but also the earth as a finely tuned, self-regulating system which supports the origin and development of life. He goes on to discuss the emergence of consciousness and the significance of human beings as observers of the very processes, in time and space, which have produced them. All of this leads him to argue that, 'the simplest explanation of what seem like extraordinary coincidences is that matter orders itself in a way that is optimal for life by the personal will of an omniscient and infinite God.'[25]

Another aspect of this interest then is the *order* displayed by such a finely-tuned universe and the *laws* which appear to underlie it. These are, naturally, of interest to scientists as observation, analysis and prediction depend on an ordered universe governed by definite laws. Professor Polkinghorne has pointed out often enough that science *assumes* the intelligibility of the world, that it is open to rational enquiry. Such an enquiry is governed by the basic laws of nature which are a 'given' for science in that they are read out from nature. They provide the basic data in terms of which science then attempts to answer questions posed by the world's processes. Although the world of Newtonian laws has disappeared, the cosmos remains ordered so that we can study it and admire it. Simplicity and elegance characterize the fundamental laws of nature, even for quantum physicists! According to Polkinghorne, the world such as this calls for a deeper explanation than the usual response: these laws are just 'brute' facts which we must assume but cannot explain![26]

Davies, similarly, claims that there are laws 'out there', transcending the physical universe. Such laws cannot even be said to have come into being with the universe, because then they could not account for its *origin*. A more profound explanation is needed and may be found in the God who necessarily creates a universe which is both subject to laws and free in terms of process. God is responsible for ordering the world by providing the various potentialities which the world is then free to make actual. In this way, the 'openness' of the universe is not compromised. Examples of this interaction between the necessary and the contingent, law and freedom may be found in the 'progressive' nature of biological evolution and in the tendency of the universe to organize itself into more and more complex forms. Of both we can say, it is not necessary that certain things should happen, but if they happen, they must happen according to the fundamental laws of nature.[27]

For both Steiner and the scientists then, it is the world's intelligibility to our enquiry which leads to questions about the transcendental basis of this interaction. At the very time, however, when physical scientists are abandoning the mechanistic paradigm, it seems to have been taken up by some life scientists. Whether it is in the insistence that the beauty and complexity of life can be *fully* explained in terms of random mutation being acted on by natural selection or in the 'astonishing hypothesis' that the human 'mind' or 'soul' is *no more* than neurological processes, there seems to be a reductionism based on the physical paradigm. Everything can be reduced to the material and no other categories of existence need be involved, even if matter must now be held to possess some very curious properties![28]

The 'anthropic principle', discussed earlier, leads us to consider that without the 'finely-tuned' precisions and balances of the universe, we would not have been here to observe the universe. Such a perspective does not *compel* us to take a teleological position but it does not exclude such a possibility. Just as cosmologists are preparing to reconsider the question of teleology or design from a fresh point of view, some life scientists, departing, it seems, from Charles Darwin's intention, are denying the idea of origin in a creator and the possibility of teleology, at least in biology.

Richard Swinburne has pointed out that even if we accept that the universe is 'a machine for making animals and humans', we can still, quite legitimately, ask whether the existence and functioning of such a machine has a further explanation. Referring to Paley's notorious metaphor of 'the watch on the heath' and to Dawkins' refutation of Paley's argument, he says, 'The watch may have been made with the aid of some blind screwdrivers (or even a blind watchmaking machine), but they were guided by a watchmaker with some very clear sight.'[29] In fact, the idea of teleology cannot be wholly excluded from the study of life and we find that in the work of even the most sceptical scientists, teleological categories creep back into the discourse.[30] Indeed, in the work of even the most reductionist, there is a sense of awe and wonder at the mystery of a complex and ordered universe. This must provide religious believers with *some* hope that dialogue, even with this constituency, is a possibility and may bear fruit.

In his book, *God and the New Physics*, Paul Davies both begins and ends with the claim that 'science offers a surer path than religion in the search for God.'[31] For John Polkinghorne this marks not only the *revival* of natural theology but its *revision*. It is now not theologians who are engaging in this exercise but scientists themselves and often, like Davies, scientists who are not always sympathetic to conventional religion. They are aware, because of their work, 'that there is more to the world than meets the eye'. Their work seems to point beyond itself, and science cannot answer all the questions raised by scientific research. More and more, scientists are recognizing the wonder of the universe, its tightly knit character and its intelligibility which makes science possible in the first place. Such a revived and revised natural theology has somewhat different concerns from its predecessors in other ages. It is not so much concerned with *particular occurrences*, such as the development of the human eye, but with the *laws and principles* which appear to underlie the existence of the universe. Science cannot investigate such laws and principles but has to assume them as 'givens' if its work is to make any progress. It is this realization which brings scientists back to the question of teleology.[32]

Polkinghorne has himself pointed out that natural theology and its insights need to be integrated into the totality of the theological enterprise. Newbigin too is acutely conscious that a wedge should not be driven between reason and revelation at this point. The self-revealing God reveals his nature and purposes in a variety of ways and it is quite possible 'to discern the evidences of his presence and work through the daily experience of the created world'. This should not, however, lead to autonomy for reason or for natural theology. Just as it is possible to know everything about a person through scientific analysis, so it is possible to know about God through nature. Neither of these procedures, however, need result in a *personal encounter*. Natural theology, then, with all its limitations, should lead towards and be consistent with a personal encounter with the God who reveals himself in history, in the prophets and definitively, of course, in Jesus Christ. Such an encounter, moreover, has to take place in relation to the community which keeps alive the memory of God's revelation in the past and makes an encounter with this God possible in the present.[33] It is well to heed Newbigin's warning about putting too much weight onto natural theology. In both the distant and the recent past, it has led to theological deism such that even the *possibility* of God's action and revelation in this world of 'changes and chances' has been denied. The wonder of the world which reminds us of God the creator and sustainer has to be held together with the wonder of God's revelation in history. The two together provide us with the possibility of a fully-orbed theology.

We have seen then the pervasiveness of belief in a Supreme Being in many religious traditions, both 'primal' and 'revealed'. We have noted also that sometimes such a belief is present in a tradition, even though the metaphysical system undergirding the tradition militates against it. We have been made aware that the question of God is a live one for many in the worlds of art, literature and the sciences. From time to time, we have been able to discern the connections between such beliefs and Christian faith.

Connections?

There are, nevertheless, some who say that there are no connections at all: those who would dismiss belief in a Supreme Being in another faith as merely an 'idol', conceptual or material. Indeed, there are Christians who deny that even in the so-called 'World Religions', there is any authentic knowledge of God. I am distressed again and again to hear Christians in the West, for example, refer to Allah as 'the God of the Muslims' or 'their God' as if Muslims worshipped another God. Sometimes such an expression is used to signify hostility to Islam but, at other times, it may be an attempt at misguided tolerance! It is true that such expressions sometimes arise out of ignorance. Many people do not know, for instance, that the Qu'rān claims continuity with the revelation given to the patriarchs and prophets and, indeed, to Jesus (2.136). It is interesting, in this connection, to observe that Christians living in the Muslim world would hardly ever speak or write in this way. At other times, however, such language is determined by theological presuppositions. If biblical revelation is regarded as entirely de novo, with no grounding in the cultures and world views surrounding ancient Israel, and if it is seen as strictly exclusive, limited to the people of God, with no relationship to the natural world and to the diverse spiritualities among the nations, then such language is understandable.

Any realistic assessment of the world's religions would have to recognize both continuities and discontinuities in this area. Even if we recognize that there is something common between them, we also have to recognize important differences. The necessarily impersonal absolute of advaita Vedanta is not identical, in every respect, with the personal God of the Bible and the Qu'rān. In the same way, while Islam has a view of God's patience, there can be no question of God suffering in, with and for his creation. For Christians, on the other hand, both the doctrines of the Incarnation and of the Atonement involve belief in a God who allows himself, out of love, to enter the human condition and to suffer with and for us.[34]

For some, the dissimilarities between Islam and Christian faith are so fundamental that they cannot arrive at an estimate of God in Islam which recognizes continuity between it and the biblical view. Kenneth Cragg, on the other hand, while recognizing that there are significant differences in the way Muslims and Christians speak about God, feels that there are also significant continuities and similarities. God is truly the *subject* of each discourse but the *predicates* used of God may differ. In conversations between Muslims and Christians, it is often the case that both parties can affirm together *some* of God's attributes (for example, his omnipotence, omniscience and mercy), while disagreeing about others (such as suffering, humility and incarnation). Cragg admits that the disagreement affects the view of each side regarding the subject but it is obvious for him that this is *disagreement regarding the one subject.*[35]

This may well be true of relations between the Abrahamic faiths, but the question remains as to the extent of disagreement about God which is possible without jeopardizing our understanding that we are referring to the same being. There is no neat, a priori answer to such a question. It is in dialogue that an answer has to be teased out and, from time to time, Christians will have to make particular judgements without foreclosing on further dialogue and greater knowledge which may cast new light on this important area of belief. Throughout, they will be concerned to understand matters of ultimate concern to their neighbours and to relate such concerns to what they know of the God of creation and redemption, of history and of science, of culture and of knowledge, of justice and of peace.

> Him neither sanctuary nor temple can contain,
> Who to his lovers comes again and again!
>
> (Iqbàl)[36]

3

In Diverse Manners

*

Most traditions that have a belief in a Supreme Being also possess, sometimes quite developed, beliefs about mediation and intercession. These 'mediators' are supposed to make human communities aware of the spiritual realm and, conversely, intercede on behalf of humans with the spiritual powers. Mbiti refers us to the intermediaries of African traditional religions. They may be living human beings such as priests, kings, oracles, medicine men, etc., or they may be the spirits of ancestors and heroes. They may also be non-human spirits or 'divinities'.[1] These last are often identified with a site or an object and, in modern African thought, are usually explained as personifications of the Supreme Being. We have noted also Bediako's criticism of some African and other theologians that they have neglected the sheer multiplicity inherent in African spirituality. He observes, however, that in West African religion, at least, both divinities and ancestors act as intermediaries between God and the human world.[2]

A Mediator between God and the World

In Hindu thought too, attempts have been made to bridge the gulf between the phenomenal world and Brahman, the transcendent absolute which is, nevertheless, the ultimate cause of the universe. If Brahman were *not* the world's cause, this would mean that it was not the absolute! At the same time, Brahman is pure silence and consciousness, being without relatedness. Its bliss (or *ananda*) is that of plenitude and it needs nothing to complete this bliss. It is here that *Ishwara* is introduced. *Ishwara* is the externalization, the personal aspect, of Brahman, responsible for the world's creation and its return to Brahman the absolute. In its self-sufficiency and unrelatedness, Brahman cannot create the world or cause it to return. *Ishwara* however, as a spilling-over of Brahman's plenitude, brings the world into being and seeks to return it to its origin. *Ishwara* is then the relational and personal aspect of Brahman, and is the object of human devotion and worship.[3]

The problem of relating the absolute to the phenomenal world is not, of course, unique to Hinduism: the world requires an explanation outside of itself, and its contingency requires grounding in necessity. But, as Keith Ward has asked, why should a necessary being create a contingent world? Surely, necessity should flow from necessity? Why, moreover, should a self-sufficient being create at all? It seems an arbitrary and pointless exercise.[4]

Process thought has sought to provide an answer by holding that God is necessary in his existence and even that he might create necessarily, but that part of the nature of this creation is openness and indeterminism. In other words, that it is in God's nature to create an evolving and developing universe which he can direct but does not coerce.[5] Even so, questions remain about *how* God orders such a universe and *how* his purposes are fulfilled in it.

Questions about God's relationship with the world and with human communities arise in a wide variety of contexts and it is worth noting that traditions which have a strongly personal view of God, based on revelation, face this question just as much as 'natural' or 'philosophical' traditions. In order *both* to safeguard God's transcendence *and* to reflect on divine self-communication, language was often developed in such a way that God's 'word', his 'wisdom' or his 'presence' came to be spoken of in personal and mediatorial terms.

In the Hebraic tradition, for example, the term *Dabar* simply means 'word' and is, more especially, used of God's Word. Already, however, in the Psalms, the term is being used to celebrate the creative power of God's Word. This Word is not just that which reveals God or enjoins conduct of a certain kind among his people, it is the very agent of creation itself. Anderson points out, in relation to Psalm 33, that this psalm was used at the time of the great autumnal festival when both creation and salvation were remembered and re-enacted. The Word not only creates but also heals or saves (Psalm 107.20).[6] By the time of the prophets, 'the Word of the Lord' was being thought of in a very personified way (Isaiah 55.11; Jeremiah 23.29). Perhaps even more interestingly, in the Targums, the Aramaic paraphrases of the Hebrew Bible, the term *Memra* (or Word) was used as a circumlocution for the tetragrammaton (or the unpronounceable divine name).

Hellenistic Judaism was well-prepared, therefore, to encounter the Heraclitean and Stoic Logos understood as the universal reason governing and permeating the world. Just as human beings have the power to deliberate or to reason and then to act in such a way as to give concrete form to their reasoning, so also the world is the result of God's thought or deliberation (it may be worth remarking here that the Hebrew and Arabic roots of *Dabar* already have this connotation). Barrett remarks, in this connection, that the thought of the Jewish philosopher, Philo, was not only influenced by stoical ideas but that he was in close touch with the biblical cosmogony, where creation is brought about by God's powerful Word.[7] Barrett notes also the strong affinities which at least some of Philo's writings have with New Testament concerns. Chief among them, is his understanding of the Logos as an intermediary between God and humanity. This same Word both pleads with the Immortal as suppliant for afflicted mortality and acts as ambassador of the ruler to the subject.[8]

The Aramaic term *Memra* is closely connected to the Arabic *Amr* which means, in Islamic terms, not only the divine command by which the world has come into being and by which it is sustained at every moment, but also that which makes God's will known to human beings. In Qu'rānic pneumatology, the Spirit of inspiration also proceeds from the divine *Amr* (17.85).[9] The Qu'rān repeatedly associates the creative Word of God with the command '*Kun*' or 'Be', and immediately 'it is' or '*fayakun*'. The creative Word of God is associated not only with the original creation but also with the final resurrection (2.117; 16.40). From the Christian point of view, it is interesting to note that it is also used of the conception of Jesus (3.59). The modern commentator Yusuf Ali says in this connection, 'God's "Word" is, in itself, the Deed. God's Promise is, in itself, the Truth. There is no interposition of Time or Condition between his Will and its consequences, for He is the Ultimate Reality. He is independent of the proximate or material causes, for He Himself creates them and establishes their laws as He pleases.'[10]

Some modern Muslim thinkers, such as Allama Iqbal, have held that the universe is a free creative movement, issuing from the innermost being of God. It is not static but is ever-growing. Reality is not something given and ready-made, it is a continuing process of becoming. The Qu'rān teaches that God is active in creation and is constantly adding to it (55.29; 35.1). The creative word of God is then not just about the original creative act and the final, eschatological act, it is what sustains and enhances creation at every moment of its being. Iqbal is here drawing very close to Process thought. Indeed, it might be said that such interpretations of Islamic teaching owe something to the stimulus of Process thought and of the philosophy of personal idealism, both of which were well-known to Iqbal.[11] In verse, he sums it up in this way:

> The universe is perhaps still unfinished,
> For the cry 'Be' and 'it is' comes with every breath completed.[12]

Also, in Christian thought, the implications of the eternity of the Word lead to the recognition of its divinity: if the Word is eternal, the Word must be God, for there cannot be another eternal besides God. This has not happened, and cannot happen, with the doctrine of the Eternal Qu'rān. We are left, therefore, with the unsatisfactory situation of two 'eternals'. Traditional theology has tried to explain this in different ways but with limited success.

It was, perhaps, considerations such as these which led to the development of a 'created *Logos*' theology and its application not to the book but to the Prophet. Although the Qu'rān does not claim anything more of the Prophet than that he was just that (and an Apostle, i.e. sent by God – 3.144), later devotion came to see him as existing before creation and, indeed, as the cause of creation. In popular devotion he is accorded quasi-divine honours and is treated as a mediator and interceder with God.[13]

This brings us back to the felt need for mediation and intercession among human beings. In a wide variety of religious and cultural contexts, we have seen that humans need ancestors, spirits, saints and prophets as mediators between themselves and the Supreme Being. The details of such mediation and intercession are variously worked out, and in some systems are more elaborate than in others, but their existence is well-nigh universal. To what extent is such mediation and intercession the result of awe and fear of the Supreme Being who is far above all that we can ask or think? In other words, is the felt need for a mediator about 'the inaccessibility of God' or has it more to do with the perception that the Supreme Being must have a purpose for creatures and that this purpose is communicated to them through mediators who can also intercede for their weaknesses (rather like Philo's *Logos*)? Is it more about the need for humans to experience divine self-communication?

It is well-known that the Qu'rān is regarded as the eternal or uncreated Word of God by Muslims. The roots of such belief are in the Qu'rān itself which refers to the 'Mother of the Book' and to the 'Preserved Tablet'. It may well be, however, that such a belief developed in the context of encounter with Christians who spoke of Jesus Christ as the incarnation of God's Eternal Word. It has often been pointed out that if such is the case, it is the Qu'rān and not the Prophet of Islam which is the true counterpart in Islam to the incarnate Christ.

At first a distinction was made between the heavenly Qu'rān and its earthly copy which was received piecemeal or in stages (17.106; 76.23). Gradually, however, this distinction disappeared and the orthodox view came to be that the written and recited book in Arabic is identical in being and reality with the uncreated and eternal Word of God. The nature of the Qu'rān itself, however, leaves us with some questions about such a view. There is, first of all, the Qu'rān's modesty. It does not claim to recount or to recapitulate all that God has ever revealed, let alone what he has chosen not to reveal (4.164; 40.78). Secondly, there is the undoubted reality that parts at least of the Qu'rān constitute a running commentary on the affairs of the Prophet of Islam and of his nascent community. This is difficult to reconcile with the doctrine that the written book is identical in every respect with the heavenly.

In Christian thought, moreover, the Logos or the Eternal Word, is seen as active in creation, revelation and redemption. It is more difficult to see a book, however exalted in nature, as an *agent* unless it is identified with God's creative Word. It is not certain, however, that such an identification is made in orthodox theology. As we have seen, God's creative Word '*kun*' continues the task of creation, bringing new things into being. The Book, on the other hand, is conceived very much in a 'once for all' way without possibility of change.

In the African context, both Bediako and Mbiti allow, in effect, that the desire for intermediaries arises in traditional religions

35

because humanity is seen as weak and sinful and needs protection and assistance if it is to approach the holiness of God. Mbiti remarks that such a view is related to social etiquette in traditional societies. Just as one would normally approach the king or a chief through someone else, so God is approached through divinities, ancestors or heroes.[14] The similarities with the hagiology of mediaeval Christendom are obvious.

Jesus Christ: the True Ancestor

Both Mbiti and Bediako have developed a theology of *anakephalaiosis* or recapitulation which sees Jesus Christ as the final and completing element that crowns the traditional religiosity of the African and brings its flickering light to full brilliance. Without Christ, African religions are incomplete. In terms of 'intermediaries', this means that Christ sums up in himself all that is believed about these intermediaries. Divinities are no longer necessary as he is the true and definitive manifestation of the Living God. Even ancestors are no longer needed as a source of blessing. In the traditional world view, spiritual power is fragmented and so is the human response; but now, in Christ, God's saving activity is focused and mediated through the Holy Spirit. Christ is the True or Primal Ancestor both in the cosmic sense of being the principal agent of creation (Colossians 1.15–20) and in the sense of being the progenitor and perfector of the community of faith (Hebrews 12.2).[15] Bediako, in particular, insists that this leaves room for ancestors not as quasi-divinities or intermediaries but as human beings who are related to Christ just as we are.[16] For him a theology of ancestors is a corollary of the continuity of God in the African experience. If the God and Father of Jesus Christ is the one who has been anticipated in traditional spirituality, then it is to be expected that he has not left himself without testimony. This does not mean simply endorsing all that happened in the past but, in the light of the Gospel, to discern carefully where and how and by whom the Gospel has been anticipated. This will lead to the discovery of the 'faithful ancestors' commemorated, for example, in the liturgy of the Church of the Province of Kenya.[17] The scope of such an understanding can be extended or limited depending on our view of how the Gospel has been anticipated. However such

ancestors are discerned, they will be seen as belonging, with us,
to the Communion of Saints.[18]

> O God of our ancestors,
> God of our people,
> Before whose face the human generations
> pass away;
> we thank you that in you we are kept
> safe for ever,
> and that the broken fragments of our
> history are gathered up in the redeeming
> act of your dear Son, remembered in this
> holy sacrament of bread and wine.
>
> (*Post-Communion prayer from the Kenyan Liturgy*)[19]

Incarnation: Divine Translation?

If Christ is seen as the only mediator in whom all human aspirations
for mediation are summed up, we are still left with the question as
to *how* Christ is such a mediator. In particular, we have to be
careful that views of Christ's mediatorship do not simply endorse
widespread cultural assumptions about God's inaccessibility.
Bishop John V. Taylor has shown how, at certain times in Christian
history, the Church has been guilty of colluding with beliefs which
would maintain God's distance from all that is 'bleared, smeared
with toil'. He sees this collusion especially in the development of
the Christian doctrine of Jesus Christ as the incarnation of the
Logos. The Logos was seen by Platonists of all kinds as an
emanation of the Absolute. The Absolute remained unmoved and
unrelated, while the Logos was thought of as the author of order in
creation and in human society. This is, of course, not dissimilar to
Hindu ideas about *Brahman* and *Ishwara*, as we have seen.

Taylor's point is that the application of such thinking about the
Logos to the event of Christ meant often that Christ as the Eternal
Word was seen on the creation side of things rather than on the
divine. Some of the early Fathers wrote as if the Logos had been
begotten to make creation possible! Such thinking and writing was,
of course, grist to the Arian mill. For Taylor, however, the
incarnate Word (as, indeed, the Holy Spirit) is intrinsic to God's
being and reveals God's nature to us. He is, moreover, concerned to

maintain both God's transcendence and his immanence. The eternal God is inwardly present to each instant of everything's existence. Not as something additional but as the Ground and Source of its being. Such a God expresses this identification with creation in a particular and unique way in the incarnation, but this only serves to manifest divine involvement, not distance. God's mind or reason, as revealed in the incarnate Word, not only shows us something of God's love and his purposes for the world, but also manifests God as he is himself. Taylor understands such a revelation in terms of 'translation'. God taking on humanity does not mean that God ceases to be what he is essentially. It is, rather, an expression of his nature. The analogies used here are of a poem that is translated into another language or an arrangement of a musical composition which yet retains the integrity and the intention of the original.[20]

Personal Encounter with God

John Taylor has himself written of the Spirit's mediatorial role and has spoken of the 'Ground of our meeting' as a most appropriate metaphor for God.[21] That is precisely the nub; it is not sufficient to think of God as underlying and permeating the whole universe. Our whole being cries out for *personal encounter* with the one who makes all personal encounters possible. However we think of the incarnation, whether in terms of 'God coming down from heaven', 'the divine taking up humanity' or the metaphor of translation, suggested by Taylor, it is this personal encounter with God in Jesus which is at the heart of the mystery.

The incarnation is the definitive form of the personal encounter with the divine who is both transcendent and immanent. This is not to say, of course, that such a personal encounter cannot be experienced elsewhere. Indeed, it can. Consider the children of Israel who experienced it at Sinai as holiness and love. Think of how God addressed his people through the prophets. Here too they realized that God's love and holiness could be experienced as grace and salvation or as wrath and judgement. It depended very much on the people's response to the prophetic message. Outside the Judaeo-Christian tradition, but closely related to it, is the example of the early, theistic Sufis in Islam. Al-Ghazzali's intense personal experience of God turned him away from scholasticism and legalism towards piety and mysticism.[22] Both Margaret Smith and Sir Norman Anderson were fascinated with the figure of Rabi'a Al-Addawiyya, the celebrated woman mystic of Islam. Rabi'a's deep love and longing for God also led to a great sense of her own sin and the need for a repentance which was not just cultic posturing.[23]

Further afield, we find in the work of the Tamil *Alvars* (Vaishnavite holy men) a strong emphasis on a personal God who is experienced as loving and gracious. What is more, these *Alvars* are known to have influenced Christian devotion as it is expressed in Tamil lyrical poetry.[24] In much of this experience of a personal God there is both a sense of God's love and graciousness and a very real sense of fear. Al-Ghazzali and Rabi'a are certainly aware of God's love but, at times, it feels as if the driving force of their spirituality is *fear*. The experience of the numinous is *mysterium tremendum et fascinans*: it is an experience of both fear and love. Such an experience of awe or of fear is often associated with the holiness and 'otherness' of God. This is true, but it also has to do with an awareness of human sinfulness and unworthiness in the presence of a God who is not only holy in the cultic sense but is righteous (*saddiq*) and just (*shaphat*). Such a God also demands righteousness and justice from human beings. The profound sense of human evil and of the human capacity for destruction which so pervades literature and the media in our times are signs of our alienation from the divine life which is our source and ground. There is a need then for reconciliation, for 'at-one-ment', for peace with God so that we may have peace within and peace with our neighbours.

John Taylor has written of his understanding of the Trinity as the Self-giver, eternally fulfilled in the giving, the Given Self, fulfilled in obedience to the will and purpose of the Giver and the 'In-othered' Self, affirming and indwelling, fulfilled in the self-giving. He understands the second of these, the Given Self, as always responding to the Father's love, always obedient to the Father's will. In the incarnation, we have, played out in history, what the Son is eternally in relation to the Father.[25] This is perfectly correct, of course, but it is more than that. In this becoming human of God the Word, we also have the re-creation of humanity. The eternal obedience of God the Word has to do also with the obedience of the man Jesus. It is this which brings the alienation between God and ourselves to an end. It is this which brings reconciliation and peace between God and humanity and, as a

result, between human beings. God's manifestation in the 'flesh'
has changed the destiny of that 'flesh' for ever.

We can speak in even an obscure and fragmentary way of the
love between the persons of the Blessed Trinity only because that
love has overflowed into the world and into our hearts (Romans
5.1–11). This love is given *generously* and without merit on our
part. This love is given *sacrificially* so that we may be healed and
restored. This love is given *triumphally* so that we may have hope
for ourselves and for the world. Any understanding of Christ's
work in his Passion, Cross, Resurrection and Ascension has to take
this self-giving love as its point of departure.

Ichabod: the Glory has Passed

Throughout the ages, in many cultures and even in particular
religious systems, there has often been an awareness that somehow
a primal harmony in the universe has been disrupted. The poet
Wordsworth, even though a great admirer of natural beauty, had to
acknowledge that there was something wrong:

> Waters on a starry night
> Are beautiful and fair;
> The sunshine is a glorious birth:
> But yet I know where'er I go,
> That there hath passed away a glory from the earth.
>
> (W. Wordsworth)[26]

This disruption is seen sometimes in nature itself; the waste and
the violence of nature, 'red in tooth and claw'. It is also seen in the
moral bankruptcy of human societies and of individuals and in the
ecological disasters that they have brought about because of their
greed or aggression. At the same time, there is a deep longing for
this harmony to be restored; what is sometimes called 'a nostalgia
for paradise'. In many traditions, this longing for harmony to be
restored is expressed in the cult and especially in the ritual of
sacrifice. It is not necessary, of course, for this to be animal
sacrifice. It is possible to have sacrifice in the form of cereals or
libations of wine and oil. Animal sacrifices do, however, play an
important part in the ritual to restore harmony. This may be
because such sacrifices enable humans to come to terms with what
they fear most in a rebellious universe. Fears of violence, blood and

death are externalized in animal sacrifice and give humans a sense of control over what they fear most. Nor can we ignore the fact that sacrifice in traditional societies has to do with property, with what is precious. In pastoral societies this was obviously animals. It also had to do with eating together, in the presence of the divinity, as a sign of the restored harmony.

Among the Hebrew prophets, however, there began to emerge a perception that God's holiness has not only to do with the correct performance of cultic ritual. The God of Israel also demands right conduct. In fact, the ethical has priority over the cultic and if the cult does not give rise to moral awareness, so much the worse for the cult!

> 'I hate, I despise your feasts,
>   and I take no delight in your solemn assemblies.
> Even though you offer me your burnt offerings and
>   cereal offerings,
>   I will not accept them,
> and the peace offerings of your fatted beasts
>   I will not look upon.
> Take away from me the noise of your songs;
>   to the melody of your harps I will not listen.
> But let justice roll down like waters,
>   and righteousness like an ever-flowing stream.'
> Amos 5.21–4, RSV (cf. Isaiah 1.11–17; Hosea 6.6; Micah 6.6–8)

The prophets are here in agreement with the psalmist when he declares: 'The sacrifice acceptable to God is a broken spirit; a broken and contrite heart, O God, thou wilt not despise' (Psalm 51.17). The prophetic call for justice and righteousness, even if this meant challenging the dominant cult, certainly resulted in suffering for the prophets. Cragg sees the Isaianic servant songs as arising from this prophetic experience of rejection and persecution because of their faithfulness to God's word. In this taking on of evil for the sake of dealing with it, we can see the emergence of the idea of moral obedience as self-sacrifice. A sacrifice, moreover, which stands in place of a rebellious people interceding for them and working for *their* repentance and salvation. It is right, of course, to see in this intimations of the messianic.[27]

4

Christ Has Died:
Redemptive Suffering

*

The Hebrew Bible speaks not only of the sufferings of God's witnesses but *of God himself*. He is seen as suffering because of the rebelliousness of his people and is pictured by the prophets in different ways: as a wronged husband whose wife has been unfaithful, for example, or as the grieving father of disobedient children. In this respect the Hebraic view of God is quite different from the Greek which held to *apatheia*, the inability to suffer, as a leading characteristic of God. God cannot be affected or limited by anything other than himself.

Christ Has Died!

If Jesus Christ is seen as the manifestation of God the Word in a human being, then his suffering and death will have to be seen not only as the suffering of a human life completely obedient to God's will but as the suffering of God himself. Both the kerygmatic speeches in the Acts of the Apostles and the letters of St Paul clearly associate God with the crucified Jesus. Peter's speech in Solomon's Portico, for instance, says 'you killed the author of life' (Acts 3.15) – and St Paul speaks of the crucifixion of 'the Lord of glory' (1 Corinthians 2.8). Early in the second century, the Bishop and martyr, Ignatius of Antioch, refers to 'the passion of our God' (Romans 6.3), echoing Acts 20.28. Even the comparatively late 'Tome of Leo', written in preparation for the Council of Chalcedon, puts it clearly, '...the only begotten Son of God was crucified and buried in accordance with that saying of the Apostle 'for had they known, they would not have crucified the

Lord of Majesty.'[1] The insertion of the phrase 'who was crucified for us' in the Trisagion by the followers of Cyril of Alexandria makes liturgical use of this belief. So the Trisagion in the Coptic Liturgy of St Basil reads:

> Holy God, Holy and Mighty, Holy and Immortal;
> Who was born of the Virgin,
> have mercy on us.
> Holy God, Holy and Mighty, Holy and Immortal;
> who was crucified for our sake,
> have mercy on us.
> Holy God, Holy and Mighty, Holy and Immortal;
> who arose from the dead and ascended to the heavens,
> have mercy on us.
>
> (St Basil)[2]

Affected by Hellenistic ideas, however, Christians in both later antiquity and in mediaeval times began to restrict Christ's suffering to his *bodily nature*, denying that the divine nature could suffer at all. If the first view, that God suffered in the flesh, could lead to monophysitism (i.e. the assertion that Christ had only one nature – the divine), the second led inevitably to Nestorianism (which tended to separate the divine and human natures in Christ, seeing their union as that of divine 'good pleasure' alone). For those who took the second view, it was quite possible to speak only of the divine or of the human nature. Nestorius and his followers were accused of believing that it was only the man Jesus who suffered, the impassible Logos remaining untouched by this suffering. In this respect, it is interesting to note that Muslim rulers often favoured the Nestorians over other Christians because they had only crosses and not crucifixes, and because they denied that God had suffered in the flesh.[3] Indeed, some scholars have gone so far as to claim that the Christology found in the Qu'rān has close affinities with Nestorian beliefs about Christ.[4]

John Taylor has pointed out that squeamishness in speaking about 'the suffering of God' in Christ was not confined to the Nestorians; it was much more widespread than that. In particular, it seems to have been ingrained in the Western theological tradition and is based, in the end, on the 'separation' of the two natures. This is illustrated by the debates about the real presence of Christ in the Eucharist which took place among the reformers. Luther, for instance, could continue to insist on the real presence of the body and blood of Christ in the bread and wine because of the ancient doctrine of *communicatio idiomatum* which teaches that what can be said of the divine nature of Christ can also be said of the human and vice versa. The human nature can be present in the eucharistic elements because it shares in the ubiquity of the divine nature. Other reformers, such as Zwingli and Calvin, denied that even Christ's glorified body could share in a divine attribute like ubiquity. It was illogical to believe that something finite could have an attribute which implied infinity. If Christ was present at all, he was present spiritually. This 'separation' of the two natures is found, for example, in the so-called 'Black Rubric' of the BCP which denies adoration to the eucharistic elements on the grounds that 'the natural Body and Blood of our Saviour Christ are in Heaven, and not here; it being against the truth of Christ's natural Body to be at one time in more places than one'.[5] With such a Christology, it is possible to hold with the Nestorians that 'only the humanity suffered' and with Aquinas that Christ was willing for 'his bodily nature' to suffer.

Bishop Taylor has shown, however, that even when Greek influence was at its height and even among those who were most under it, a sense of the biblical witness to the suffering of God remained. Some of the Fathers (including Origen) spoke not only of the suffering of the incarnate Word but of the Logos in all ages and all places, and even of the Father's suffering.[6]

Throughout the Christian era there has been an acute tension between the Hebraic and the Hellenistic views of God. The Hellenistic view of God as inaccessible, impassible and immutable confronts the biblical view where God is certainly unchangeable in his faithfulness, but also suffers because of his love for his creatures, judges them because of their sinfulness and forgives them when they repent. The tension is well illustrated by the different ways in which the Greek tradition and Christian theology have understood the term 'impassibility'. The Greeks have held that God cannot be acted on from outside and that he cannot change within himself. It is true that this doctrine has been very influential in Christian thought, even to the point where it is confused with the Christian doctrine.[7] Strictly speaking, however, the Christian doctrine is *not* that God cannot suffer but that he cannot be *made* to suffer. Insofar as God enters into suffering, he does so freely and by his own deliberate decision. Even such a limited view of impassibility is under challenge from various quarters and for different reasons. If God creates necessarily, because it is his nature to create, and this is 'the best of all possible worlds', because God's goodness demands that it should be, then a certain amount of suffering is necessary. The witness of the Bible, indeed of all theistic religion, is that God is not unmoved by the suffering of his creatures, but is working to heal and to save. The Doctrine Commission puts it like this:

> The only ultimately satisfactory response to the problem of unmerited or disproportionate suffering is to believe that our Creator, through a wonderful act — at once of self-limitation and of self-expression, is present in the darkest affliction, shares our pain, bears our sorrows, and sustains us through it all, creating good in spite of evil, so revealing the true nature of divine power as showing mercy and pity.[8]

Suffering is at the very heart of the divine Being.

The Cross Reveals God as He Is

'Only a suffering God can help,' said Bonhoeffer and this God is seen supremely in the self-giving love of the Cross. Among the reformers, Martin Luther is significant because of his emphasis on a theology of the Cross (*theologia crucis*) by which he meant not only an understanding of the atonement but a view of the whole of theology as a theology of the Cross. The Cross truly reveals God as he is and must, therefore, be at the basis of all thought about God. It is well-known that Luther contrasts his *theologia crucis* with the *theologia gloriae* of much mediaeval theology which laid stress on God's power, wisdom and goodness as they could be discerned in both creation and revelation. Luther does not deny that the created world provides evidence of God but this knowledge is not sufficient for salvation. It is the suffering, shame and humiliation of the Cross which reveal the Creator as also the Redeemer: One who is involved in the pain and suffering of the world and who is bringing it to a good end. Such an appreciation of the Cross is not 'natural' for sinful humanity which prides itself on its intellectual and spiritual powers. It can only come about because by God's grace our eyes of faith are opened and we can see the significance of God's 'hidden work' on the Cross. The Cross reveals the true glory of God in his willingness to suffer in, with and for his creatures. In this sense the *theologia crucis* is the authentic *theologia gloriae* (John 12.20–33).[9]

Since the conversion of Constantine and the emergence of 'Constantinian Christianity', wherever and whenever the Church has triumphed in political and social terms, God has been conceived as *Pantokrator*, Almighty, All-powerful, Omnipotent. In a spate of articles, and finally in his Hulsean Lectures, *Deity and Domination*, the late David Nicholls has drawn our attention to how the social and political milieu affects our language about God and vice versa.[10] The Doctrine Commission laments that our liturgical usage generally reflects a 'Constantinian' situation in which God is addressed as King, Judge, Lord, etc. In fact, we live in a largely 'post-Constantinian' context where such language no longer carries much credibility. The experience of tremendous human suffering in the twentieth century, not only in major global conflict but in 'little wars' throughout the world, as well as oppression and injustice on a large scale, have made a renewed theology of the Cross necessary. Such a theology has been in the process of development throughout this century, but it received a significant impetus during and after the Second World War and also with the rise of theologies of liberation. Interestingly enough, when reflection on the Cross was revived in the modern period, it was often in circles influenced by the thought of Martin Luther. This was beginning to happen already in the years between the two world wars, but it received enormous encouragement from the events of World War II.

A significant watershed, in this respect, was the publication of Kazoh Kitamori's *Theology of the Pain of God*.[11] Kitamori was writing in the context of the huge destruction of life and property brought about by the Second World War, so much of it by his own country of Japan (it is interesting, in this connection, to recall that Nagasaki, one of the two cities destroyed by the Atom Bomb, was and is a major Christian centre in Japan). With his Lutheran background and also his awareness of tragic themes in Japanese literature, Kitamori sought to understand what had happened to the Japanese people throughout the period of Japan's military adventure and its inevitable nemesis, and to reconcile this with a Christian understanding of God. Japanese awareness of human pain and tragedy which bring about renewal, should lead to a fresh understanding of pain at the deepest heart of God's being, pain which is most clearly seen in the suffering and death of 'the beloved son'. This is supremely the pain of love, bringing about redemption and leading to new life.

The theme of God's suffering love was brilliantly developed by Jürgen Moltmann in The Crucified God.[12] The Cross is to be understood as God's loving solidarity with suffering and alienated human beings. Moltmann is profoundly Trinitarian here; the Cross is not the death of God but it is death in God. It is an event in the love of God in which the Son suffers abandonment by the Father, the Father suffers in the Son's death and the Holy Spirit is the love, even in this pain, between the Father and the Son, overflowing into the world for its healing and salvation.

For liberation theologians, such as Jon Sobrino, the theological task in the context of suffering and oppression must begin with the suffering of God. There can be hope only if God is suffering with and for us, transforming the hopelessness of our situation by the power of his suffering love. A God who does not or cannot suffer can hardly be the loving creator and redeemer of a world full of suffering and pain.[13]

The Cross Reveals God's Love

Some writers have tried to relate the suffering of God to an understanding of the universe which sees it both as genuinely 'other' than God and as in the process of becoming. In the creation of such a universe, God has taken a risk because the possibilities of its going wrong exist at every stage and in many different ways. Such a risk is inherent in the creation of an autonomous and developing universe. Thinking of this kind is not new, of course, and is characteristic of the Irenaean stream of patristic thought. What is new is that the process of struggle and of perfecting is now not left just to the universe but is brought into the being of God himself. God has not only created the world but is redeeming it at every moment and in various ways. This redemption, moreover, is not the effortless recovery of an original perfection. It is struggle and suffering at the heart of God's being. In such thought, the Cross is often regarded as the most intense manifestation in history of what is happening continually in the cosmos: God's struggle in

the perfecting of a developing universe. In his famous hymn, Bill
Vanstone brings together these strands of thought in a telling way:

> Love that gives, gives evermore,
> Gives with zeal, with eager hands,
> Spares not, keeps not, all outpours
> Ventures all, its all expends.
>
> Drained is love in making full,
> Bound in setting others free,
> Poor in keeping many rich,
> Weak in giving power to be.
>
> Therefore he who shows us God
> Helpless hangs upon the tree;
> And the nails and crown of thorns
> tell of what God's love must be.[4]

The cross is not, however, simply an illustration of God's suffering
love in creation and history. It is the point at which God's will to
save and the obstinacy in the heart of the 'other' to remain 'other'
meet. The Cross is, in other words, about the rejection of God's
purposes for the world by the world itself through the agency of
creatures who are both free and conscious of their freedom. In the
words of Kenneth Cragg, 'The Cross is what happens in a world
like ours to a love like God's.'[5] Any view which regards humanity
and the world as redeemable must reckon with the depth of this
rejection.

For Christians, however, the Cross is not only revelational,
showing us God's nature and purposes. It is also *anthropological*; for
in the very rejection of the Creator by the creation, a new creation
is brought into being. Through the most radical act of human
rebellion, a new humanity is inaugurated. There *is* a sense in which
the new is a recovery of the old: in the faithful obedience of Jesus
there is a return to God's original purpose for humanity. In his
suffering and death is *recapitulated*, another Irenaean theme, the
attempted obedience of human beings at any time and in many
cultures and places. But it is not simply a recovery of the old. This
is no return to prelapsarian innocence. Sin has to be reckoned with
and the new humanity in Christ is to be both accounted righteous
before God on the basis of Christ's work and gradually made
righteous according to the righteousness of Christ. In terms of the

traditional language, the *imputation* of Christ's righteousness to us, by grace through faith, results in the *impartation* of his righteousness which becomes ours in the course of time.[16] This is not only a return to being the 'Adamic icon' (*selem*) of Genesis but a going on from that to what the apostle calls 'the measure of the stature of the fulness of Christ' (Ephesians 4.13) who is himself the 'express image' of God (Hebrews 1.3). The new humanity is both a creative act of God's and born out of human struggle in the 'working out of our salvation' (Philippians 2.12).

Such a humanity is characterized by a radical dependence on God for the very possibility of knowing him and his purposes for us. It is characterized also by a deep and continuing *metanoia*, a turning away from all that prevents fellowship with God, including cultic and legalistic aspects of religion, and a turning towards the Cross, in Word and Sacrament, so that we may receive its benefits. Such a 'turning' to God and dependence upon him bring about a metamorphosis or transformation of our inward being (Romans 12.2), so that our hearts overflow with love for God and for our neighbours. As Anna of *Mister God, This is Anna* saw very well, such transformation comes because God can 'kiss you right inside'.[17] Such an experience of acceptance by God, because of our turning to the Cross of Christ, can never remain individual. It results in the desire for the transformation of human society so that it may reflect, more and more, God's kingly rule and, indeed, in the desire for the transformation of the whole of creation so that it is liberated from its bondage to inevitable decay and is renewed according to God's purposes revealed in Jesus Christ (Romans 8.20–1; Ephesians 1.9–10).

The Cross: Paradigm and Parable

Christian thought about the Atonement can be divided into the paradigmatic and the parabolic. The paradigmatic has to do with what the Cross *is*, while the parabolic with how it is explained. If we take the paradigmatic first, we have seen that the Cross reveals something of the nature of God himself. This is why Cyril of Alexandria's insistence that God suffered for our sakes is nearer the heart of the biblical and patristic witness than the 'Nestorian' distinction between the suffering of Christ's human nature and his divine impassibility. Secondly, it is important to emphasize the humanity of Christ as the inauguration of a renewed humanity in which, according to the divine intention, all are included (Romans 11.32; Ephesians 1.10; 1 Timothy 4.10). If people turn away from the divine plan that is another matter. God's purposes, however, are universal. Because of the implications of Christ's humanity for ours, docetism of any kind is not an option. Thirdly, Christ suffered and died as our representative (and substitute, if you like). He stood in our place to do what sin had made us unable to do. God accepts this sacrifice of obedience made on behalf of all, and in the Cross there is divine reconciliation with estranged humanity (2 Corinthians 5.19). The Cross opens up the way from and to God. Those who take on the pattern of the Cross and walk in the way of the Cross experience forgiveness of sin and find strength for the future.

Sometimes the paradigmatic aspects of the Cross are confused with the parabolic. A metaphor or illustration to explain a doctrine or an event is confused with the doctrine or event itself! There are many telling parables or metaphors of Christ's death in the Bible and in Christian tradition. Let us consider, for a moment, the metaphor of 'ransom'. In the Jewish Scriptures, the term often means a covering (*kopher*) for sin or an offering of atonement. In the early Church (including the usage in the New Testament), the term *lutron* comes from the context of the sacral manumission of slaves. The custom, apparently, was that when a slave had earned enough money or had a friend who was willing to provide the money, and the slave's owner was willing, the slave would go to the temple of a particular god and the priests of the temple would purchase the slave from the owner. Technically the slave became a slave of the god but, in civil terms, this meant, in effect, freedom for the slave. In the Jewish context too, the term was used for the ransoming, by the next of kin, of an enslaved relative. New Testament expressions such as 'you have been bought with a price' (1 Corinthians 6.20), doubtless, have this background in mind. The New Testament scholar, C. E. B. Cranfield, suggests, however, that in Jesus' own use of the term in Mark 10.45, 'the Son of man . . . came . . . to give his life as a ransom for many', the suffering servant of Isaiah 53 is strongly to the fore. The idea here is not so much of sacral manumission as of the guilt offering of the Pentateuch. Jesus was thinking of himself as the Servant suffering vicariously for the sins of others.[18]

It is interesting to note in this connection that the Qu'rān too speaks of ransom in the context of sacrifice. In the story of

Abraham's readiness to sacrifice his son in obedience to God's will (the son, incidentally, is not named in this passage), the boy is ransomed by God with 'a tremendous victim'. The root of the Qu'rānic word used here is *fida* which is closely related to *pdh*, the root of one of the Hebrew words used for ransom in the Hebrew Bible.[19] In Christian tradition, of course, this story is regarded as a type of Christ's suffering and death.

Ransom, then, can be a powerful metaphor for speaking of Christ's passion in a variety of cultures and situations. It is illegitimate, however, to turn the metaphor into a literal transaction that took place on the Cross. The early and mediaeval debate, therefore, about the one to whom the ransom was paid is a misunderstanding of how the metaphor works. The primary concern here is not whether it was to God or the Devil that the ransom was paid but the *cost* of Christ's suffering for our sake and our *obligation* to Christ for this reason.

Another metaphor that had currency, particularly in the Middle Ages, is that of the satisfaction of divine honour. Human sin had offended against divine honour and there had to be punishment so that this honour could be vindicated. Christ was then seen as taking the punishment due to us for our sin and disobedience. Naturally, in a feudal and hierarchically organized society in which the concept of honour was important for society to work, this metaphor made sense and was widely used by theologians such as St Anselm, Archbishop of Canterbury. Anselm argued that such was the seriousness of sin and the inadequacy and inability of human beings to make a proper restitution for it, that a God-man is necessary to satisfy divine honour by taking the punishment due to rebellious humanity. The force of this metaphor has been greatly reduced in societies that are not so hierarchically organized and where personal or social honour does not play a significant part.[20]

A leading metaphor which occurs already in the Scriptures is that of Christ 'bearing our sins' (Isaiah 53.4; 1 Peter 2.24; etc.). The Reformers understood this as taking the penalty due to us for breaking the law. Such a 'penal substitutional' view attracts the objection that it is hardly moral to transfer penalties in this way. Also, it creates the impression that God is a merciless judge who must extract the proper penalty, even if it is not from the offender! A more contemporary re-working of this metaphor emphasizes the 'representative' nature of the Cross. Christ stands in our place to do what we cannot do. As representative *anthropos* he restores fellowship between God and ourselves through his obedience-unto-death. In this sense, he deals with sin and the penalty due to sin. In his death, the old humanity of sin dies and the new humanity of obedience and fellowship with God is born. Yet another metaphor is that of 'the harrowing of hell': once again, a metaphor like this flourished in the Middle Ages when people had vivid images of the supernatural and also great fear of supernatural evil. The 'harrowing of hell' theme in art, literature and drama was a celebration of Christ's victory over the devil and thus provided reassurance that God would indeed triumph over evil in the universe. In our own day, we still need to think of Christ's death as victory over evil but, perhaps, not quite in the same way as people in mediaeval times! For us it may be more important to focus on the evil and rebellion in our own hearts which can be overcome by the example of Christ. It may be right for us to reflect on how Christ's death deals with corruption in the 'principalities and powers' of human society, the Cross being both judgement on such corruption and salvation for society inasmuch as it is the re-creation of humanity as a whole. Christ's victory over evil is promoted by Gustaf Aulen as a classic way of understanding the Atonement, dominant in both the Scriptures and the patristic writings. Aulen is clear, however, that it is the theme or idea he is promoting, not the ancient or mediaeval ways of presenting it:

> It is, therefore, of the first importance to distinguish between the classic idea itself and the forms in which it has been expressed. Some of the forms in which it has clothed itself have been the actual provocation and the main cause of the harsh judgements which have been passed upon it; and, indeed, when the crude and realistic images which are to be found in the Fathers and in Luther are interpreted as if they were seriously intended as theological explanations of the Atonement, it is only to be expected that they should provoke disgust. But that is to miss the point. The images are but popular helps for the understanding of the idea.[21]

The Cross, the Church and the Sacraments

The Cross of Christ is the origin of the Church. If Christians are reconciled to God and to one another, and if the Church is the company of the reconciled, it is because of Christ's reconciling work on the Cross (2 Corinthians 5.18–19; Ephesians 2.16). The centrality of the Cross for the Church is seen most clearly in the dominical sacraments of Baptism and Eucharist.

Since the earliest times, baptism, the fundamental rite of initiation, has been understood as baptism into the death of Christ (Romans 6.3–4; the passage also speaks of being raised by Christ but more of that later). Baptism into Christ's death has to do with solidarity in his suffering for the sake of the world's salvation (Philippians 3.10). Our sacrifices of thanks and praise, of obedience and of service are only possible because of Christ's self-offering and it is because we enter into 'the movement of his self-offering' that our sacrifices are acceptable to God (Hebrews 13.13–17).[22]

Because baptism is solidarity with Christ, it is also solidarity with one another; with the Body of Christ (1 Corinthians 12.13). It is, therefore, the primary sacrament of unity. It is encouraging that since the process which ended in the publication of the 'Lima' text, there has been an increasing recognition among the churches that all Christians share a common baptism.[23] It is particularly significant that the Roman Catholic Church has, since the Second Vatican Council, recognized the baptism of other Trinitarian churches. This has implications for the Roman Catholic understanding of the Church. Those who have been baptized are, *ipso facto*, members of the Body of Christ, the Church, even if they are outside the Roman communion. This is why the *Decree on Ecumenism* tends to recognize the ecclesiality of other Christian churches although they are still regarded, in varying degrees, as lacking something because they are not in communion with the Bishop and the See of Rome. Pope John Paul II's encyclical *Ut Unum Sint* affirms this understanding and takes it further. According to him, the elements of sanctification and truth present in these churches lead the Roman Catholic Church to recognize that 'the one Church of Christ is effectively present in them'.[24]

Such an understanding is one of the reasons why *Lumen Gentium*, the Dogmatic Constitution on the Church, speaks of the Church of Jesus Christ as 'subsisting in' the Roman Catholic Church. More conservative elements had wanted the Council to identify the Church of Jesus Christ with the Roman Catholic Church. This would have left little room for recognizing any ecclesiality among 'the separated brethren'. Among others, this change was an important signal to the leaders of other churches that dialogue with the Roman Catholic Church could begin.[25]

The Eucharist, or the Lord's Supper, is the central act of worship of the Christian community. Christians from varying traditions are agreed that it is 'the breaking of the bread and the prayers' which characterize a Christian community. Frequent celebration of the Eucharist is not limited to those with a 'high' sacramental point of view. The Brethren emphasize the importance of it just as much as 'Parish Eucharist' Anglicans. The revival of frequent communion among Anglicans was due as much to the Evangelicals as to the Tractarians.[26] Many of the radical base communities of Latin America, deprived of the ministry of priests, are nevertheless keen to continue to celebrate the Lord's Supper, even if they know that such a form of celebration is not everything the Roman Catholic Church teaches the Eucharist to be.[27]

The Eucharist is said to be constitutive of the Church precisely because it is a memorial of the Lord's death 'until he comes'. From the earliest times, whenever Christians have gathered together to break bread, they have remembered the Passion of Christ. Biblical commentators are agreed that the Passion narrative in each of the Gospels forms the most coherent and concrete part of the tradition. It is also the point where the Gospels are most in agreement. Surely, the rehearsal of the events of the Passion at the weekly celebration of the Lord's Supper would have 'stylized' this part of the tradition in exactly the way we find it?[28]

The Sacrifice of Christ is spoken of as 'passover' in the New Testament (1 Corinthians 5.7) and the Eucharist is the Christian celebration of this passover. It is true that the roots of the Eucharist can also be traced back to other kinds of Jewish gatherings, such as the *chaburah* meals eaten together by companies of friends. The language and imagery of remembering the Lord's passover remain dominant, however, and we have to consider that every remembrance of the passover is passover itself. Remembrance now does not mean merely a memorial of a long-past event, however significant it may have been. Recent discussion of both *anamnesis* and its Hebrew equivalent *zeker* has shown that such a remembrance is a bringing to the present of what God has done in the past. In ancient literature, it is sometimes a re-enactment of a great event in history or mythology. In the context of the Eucharist, we may say that it is making Christ's once-for-all and unrepeatable sacrifice present and effective for those who partake of it (1 Corinthians 10.16–21). The sacrifice is made present for us so that we may partake of its benefits, as Luther has said.

Such an understanding of the Eucharist makes Christ's suffering and death real for us every time we come together. We are able here not only to partake of the benefits Christ has procured for us but to join ourselves and our sufferings with Christ and his suffering (Hebrews 13.13; Philippians 3.10). This should not be seen as a denial of the uniqueness of Christ's atoning death. It is, rather, the Church, as the Body of Christ, completing in itself and in individual believers the suffering of Christ (Colossians 1.24).

Throughout history Christians have been called to suffer for Christ's sake. Whenever they have obeyed God rather than human beings, whenever they have struggled for justice for the poor and oppressed, whenever they have witnessed to God's great acts of liberation, they have had to pay a penalty and, sometimes, the extreme penalty. Nor is this a matter simply in the past. Numerous Christians, in every part of the world, continue to suffer for their beliefs and for trying to work out the values of the Gospel in their daily lives and in their communities. Christian mission and development agencies, as well as campaigning groups, are continually making us aware of such suffering.

In the minds and hearts of those who suffer, their suffering is immeasurably enriched because it is understood by them to be conjoined with Christ's suffering. In such circumstances, the Eucharist is a reminder (that word again) that we truly participate in Christ's death and resurrection. Of course, it is not only in terms of our suffering that we are conjoined with Christ in the Eucharist. It is also because our prayers are 'through the merits of Jesus Christ our Saviour' (as the Book of Common Prayer puts it). Our intercessions are offered to God, pleading his sacrifice, and he intercedes for us because of his once-for-all sacrifice (Hebrews 7.25). There is a connection between his pleading for us and our pleading on the basis of his sacrifice.

> Look, Father, look on his anointed face,
> And only look on us as found in him;
> Look not on our misusings of thy grace,

Our prayer so languid, and our faith so dim:
For lo! between our sins and their reward
We set the Passion of thy Son our Lord.
(W. Bright)[29]

Although the Eucharist *is* something *we* do to praise and thank God
for the Cross of his son, it is supremely God's initiative: Christ
gives us of his benefits as an act of generosity and of grace. This
means that the impact of the Eucharist is continually transcending
the bounds and the boundaries of the institutional Church. Of
course, there must be order in the celebration of the Eucharist. It
is right that those who are authorized by the wider Church to
preside and to teach in the community, should be those who
preside at the Eucharist. It is right that the apostolic tradition is
handed on in the context of the Eucharist by those who are its
guardians. It is right also that sharing at the Lord's Table should
result in sharing other spiritual and material resources within the
community and with the wider world. Eucharistic life does,
however, break out in all sorts of unexpected places: in gatherings
of young people, among oppressed groups struggling for freedom
and justice and among Christians in 'frontier' mission and ministry.
Such eucharistic expressions may lack some of the order which the
Church, in fidelity to apostolic tradition, regards as necessary.
Many of them are, nevertheless, authentic manifestations of *agape*
love; whether that is thought of as love between Christians or as
God's love shown to us in Christ. They glorify Christ and bind
Christians together in a more intimate fellowship. As such, they
are to be gratefully received, even if it is allowed that they are not
complete expressions of the Church's beliefs about the Eucharist.

The institutional Church has also to be aware that many of these
expressions of eucharistic life appear where the Church has failed
to provide the means for a full celebration of the Eucharist. Boff
points out that the Second Vatican Council teaches the centrality of
the Eucharist for the building up of a Christian community. The
Church has, however, failed to provide sufficient numbers of
ordained ministers so that each community may be Eucharist-
centred in the way it should be. A mere 'law of the Church', the
rule of celibacy, comes up against Divine Law. Which is to prevail?
The Latin American base communities have addressed this problem
by having their lay coordinators preside at their celebrations of

'the Lord's Supper', if a priest is not available for 'mass'. These coordinators are leaders of their communities and, according to Boff, may rightly be regarded as extraordinary ministers of the Eucharist. Boff allows that something is lacking in such a celebration but he is also confident that they are a real means of sacramental grace.[30]

In the Anglican Communion too, there is sometimes a scarcity of ordained ministers. Anglicans are not, however, bound by the rule of celibacy. If there are local leaders in a Christian community who can preside in terms of worship, teaching and stewardship, there is no reason why their vocation to ordained ministry should not be tested and recognized. They may then be prepared in an appropriate way and commissioned by the wider Church. The Bishop and other stipendiary clergy will continue to exercise a ministry of *episcope* or oversight in relation to such communities and their local ministers, both ordained and lay. Whatever such schemes are called and whatever drawbacks they may have, they go a long way towards ensuring that each local community has the ministers it needs for the fullness of its corporate life.

The Cross and Principalities and Powers

The Cross of Christ liberates people from different kinds of bondage. It frees, of course, from guilt and from the sense of self-alienation which is the result of guilt. Because of the Cross we know that God loves us, has forgiven us for Christ's sake and has shown us a new way of wholeness and fulfilment. The Cross frees people from slavish adherence to custom and law. Custom, and the culture from which it springs, are not bad in themselves. Indeed, they provide the basic forms in the context of which human life can flourish. As such they are God-given and to be celebrated. Because of human sinfulness, however, customs too can become a source of oppression and tyranny, restricting the freedom of men and women. We can never forget that Jesus was crucified because he had challenged customs of his day which excluded the marginalized from the mainstream of society. When the Gospel arrives in a particular culture, some of its customs are recognized as God-given and good, others as morally and spiritually neutral and yet others as contrary to the Gospel because they diminish the humanity of the whole group or of sections or individuals within it. Christians will then wish to affirm what is God-given in a culture but they will also want to challenge whatever is contrary to God's will. People will need to be freed, in the name of Christ, from all that shackles them.[31]

Bishop Lesslie Newbigin has pointed out that the 'principalities and powers' of the New Testament may be understood as the informing principles of institutions and civilizations: the 'spirit' of a school, for instance, or the 'sovereignty' of Parliament. In themselves, these principalities and powers are good and God-given. They provide order and stability for society and, as such, reflect the ordering work of the Logos. The Letter to the Colossians tells us that these principalities and powers were created through Christ and for Christ and that they find their coherence in him (Colossians 1.15–17). They have been corrupted, however, by evil and have enslaved men and women down the ages. The ministry of Jesus was a resounding 'no' to this enslavement both for others and for himself. He was free of tradition and custom which diminished human beings and he set others free. It was this defiance which led to the Cross but the very moment of apparent triumph for evil was turned to victory for Christ. It became clear that even the threat of suffering and death could not hold him, and cannot hold us, in thrall to corrupt principalities and powers. Christ has opened up for us the way of obedience to the Father and, in doing so, has broken the hold of these powers over the human race (Colossians 2.14–15). For the Christian, the principalities and powers will be subservient to Christ and the Gospel. No loyalty, whether to nation or to ethnicity or to family will be greater than the loyalty to Christ; and the 'informing principles' of all human institutions will be tested for their coherence with the Good News in Jesus Christ.[32]

It may well be that when St Paul speaks of 'principalities and powers' he has the Law particularly in mind (Galatians 4.1–8). He would have been thinking of the Mosaic Law and the various interpretations and developments of it current in his time. It is clear that the Law is good and is from God but it has been used by those with power to lay burdens on men and women which they cannot bear (Matthew 23.4). As John Stott has put it, 'God intended that the Law should reveal our sin and drive us to Christ but Satan has used it to reveal our sin and drive us to despair.'[33]

Every society needs law for its good governance, but human

beings have a tendency to exalt law to a status it should not have. This is particularly the case with religious law. It is natural, of course, that a dominant religious tradition should influence the development of law in a particular country but this is very far from imagining that mediaeval codes of law developed in very different situations could be enforced today in their entirety. Yet this is the programme of many political movements inspired by a fundamentalist ideology.

It is clear that the battle is not with law but with legalism; the belief that detailed rules of behaviour and detailed rules for punishment, if the legal code is violated, will result in a perfect society. The preaching of the Cross, rather, is that inward conversion to God is more important than legal codes. That it is better to free people from what enslaves and oppresses them than to desire increasingly petty codes of conduct. That true fulfilment comes from a radical obedience to God which involves a right disposition. That a sacrificial life-style more truly reflects the Kingdom of God than a host of legal minutiae.

The Cross of Christ remains an inspiration for all of those who suffer because of their commitment to truth or because they have struggled against oppression and injustice, whether in the name of political or of religious ideology. It remains an inspiration for all who make sacrifices for the advancement of God's reign. Because of the Cross, they know that their struggle is meaningful and that truth and justice will prevail. Because of the Cross, they know they will be vindicated.

The Cross of Christ is about death but it is also about life beyond death. It is about death that leads to new, transformed life. This is perhaps why the Cross is so often depicted as a tree of life.

5
Christ Is Risen:
Life after Life?

*

Throughout history many religious and cultural traditions have held that the human person or 'soul' is essentially immortal. They have reflected on the inherent dignity of men and women, on their spirituality, on their power to think and on their ability to create complex civilizations. They have concluded, as a result of this, that there is a divine spark in human persons which makes them different from the rest of creation and which survives their physical dissolution.

It appears, however, that in the earliest days such was not the belief of the Hebrews. They seem to have had a very this-worldly view which was concerned about communal and individual whole-ness in this life. In this connection, it is interesting to observe the extent to which the term *shalom* is rooted in Hebrew (and, more generally, Semitic) notions of safety, completeness and welfare. If there was belief in survival after death, it was limited to a shadowy existence in *Sheol*. Such an existence was certainly not regarded as very desirable. In fact, it was to be greatly feared. Not only was it a cutting off from the land of the living, from human society, it was also supposed to have been a distancing from God (Psalm 6.5; 30.9). Although the Psalms also affirm that God's sovereignty extends to Sheol (139.8), it was only gradually that views of an afterlife, and in particular, views of resurrection, began to emerge.[1]

In some cases views of an afterlife in the Hebrew Bible and in the Apocrypha are influenced by the beliefs of surrounding peoples. The thoughts of The Preacher for instance, regarding the human spirit returning to God who made it (Ecclesiastes 12.7) may well have had Mesopotamian astral religion as its background. Similarly, the author of the apocryphal Wisdom of Solomon appears to have assimilated the Greek view of the immortality of the soul.[2] Also, in the Books of the Maccabees there are instances of prayers for the dead.

Resurrection

While Israel was certainly influenced by her neighbours in the development of belief in an afterlife, Wheeler Robinson has pointed out that this came to fuller expression in characteristically Hebraic terms. Hebrew thought tended to regard human beings as a psychosomatic unity. If the soul was deprived of the body, it could exist in only a shadowy way. For fullness of life, it needed a body and this is where the notion of resurrection emerged.[3]

It is true that one of the earliest images of resurrection is not about individual resurrection at all. It is, rather, about the communal renewal of the People of Israel (Ezekiel 37.1–14). It is clear, nevertheless, that notions of resurrection are present already. Isaiah 25.8 and 26.19 teach the abolition of death and the resurrection of the dead. They fit well into their contexts though some commentators regard them as later interpolations. Even so, they must be among the earliest references to resurrection in the Old Testament. It is well known that the book of Daniel also refers to the resurrection of the dead. It is interesting that the book of Daniel contains the most Persian 'loan words' of all the books of the Bible. It seems that while Wheeler Robinson is correct in his belief that the doctrine of the resurrection is required by Hebrew anthropology and is not an import, the impetus for the development of the doctrine may well have come from outside, perhaps during the exile. Such a view is certainly strengthened when one considers the colour and terminology of the inter-testamental apocalyptic literature. Apart from Canaanite influence, there are discernible connections with Babylonian and Zoroastrian eschatology. It is, perhaps, worth pointing out that *paradise* is a loan word in both Hebrew and Arabic, borrowed from Persian.

Establishing connections between the Bible and the beliefs of people with whom the Israelites came into contact, does not, in any way, militate against the integrity of the Bible and the truth of its teaching. An investigation into the sources of beliefs does not impugn their authenticity. In fact, it may strengthen and highlight the truth of such beliefs.

By the time of Jesus and of the early Church, we find a quite well developed language of apocalyptic and, within it, of eschatology or beliefs about the last things. Jesus himself and the writers of the New Testament were, in varying degrees, steeped in such language and ideas and used them to communicate the Good News of what God was doing through Jesus Christ. The main concerns of the New Testament, however, are moving away from those of Jewish apocalyptic back to the great universal concerns of the writing prophets: how will God reveal himself to all and how will he fulfil his purposes for the world which he has created?

The Coming of God: the Crib, the Cross and the Cave

We have seen already how the Cross came to be seen as the supreme instance of obedience to God. Jesus is the new Adam, the new humanity, not in rebellion over and against God and disrupting the universe, but reconciled to God and to his purposes in the world. The other side of the picture is that he is also the great self-revelation of God. He reveals to us that God not only *requires* sacrifice but *is* sacrifice himself. In other words, the heart of God is revealed to be cross-shaped!

Such suffering love is brought out clearly in Jesus' own parable of the two lost sons: they were both lost, one in the prodigality of his wickedness, the other in the prodigality of his self-righteousness. The father's love is shown in that he goes out to meet and to welcome both sons. At least one of them repents because of his encounter with grace. We do not know what happened to the other. Oriental commentators remind us that the father's actions are counter-cultural. No father, particularly if he were wealthy and influential, would go out to meet his sons in the street or the field. He would expect the sons to come to him. Here is a father, however, who runs out into the street, with robes trailing in the dust, who embraces and kisses a dirty vagabond and who then goes out again to entreat an obstinate and rebellious older son. Here is suffering love indeed.[4]

The father 'going out' to meet his sons, brings us close to the heart of the incarnation. God is no longer sending messengers; he has come himself (Hebrews 1.1–3). 'The Word was made flesh and dwelt among us and we beheld his glory . . .' (John 1.14).

In Anglican theological reflection, the incarnation is often held to be central. Some see this as a weakness because, for them, it obscures the centrality of the Cross. It can, however, be understood as central in the sense that everything else depends upon it. It is important to remember that those who espoused the centrality of the doctrine of the incarnation also went on to point out that such an incarnation was *kenotic*, that is self-emptying.[5] In other words, their doctrine led ultimately and inevitably to the Cross. The Cross has universal, salvific value precisely because it is the suffering of God-become-flesh. It is God doing for us what we could not do for ourselves. It is God restoring us to fellowship with him. It is God enabling us to walk in the way of the Cross.

Christ is Risen!

But if God's love is embodied in the crib and the cross, it must also be embodied in whatever caused the cave to be empty on that first Easter morning. If docetism is not an option at the crib and on the Cross, it is not an option at the empty tomb. If the Word was made flesh in the crib and if God suffered in human form on the Cross, then the raising of the dead Jesus cannot be mere 'appearance'. The empty tomb belongs to the apparatus of the incarnation. As human beings we need to experience love in an embodied way. What would human love be if, for example, it always had to be expressed at the end of a telephone line? In the same way, we need divine love to be embodied. In the first letter of St John, we are told that the early disciples had not only seen and heard such love but 'touched it and handled it' (1 John 1.1). The letters written within St Peter's circle make much the same point about the personal testimony to the apprehension of divine love (2 Peter 1.16–18). If divine love is apprehended in an embodied way in crib and cross, and everything in between, then surely it must be apprehended in the same way at that supreme moment of divine self-revelation, the resurrection of Jesus Christ from the dead? If the incarnation has any meaning, the risen Christ must be embodied. It is true, of course, that such an embodiment is not a mere resuscitation of the old body. It is a taking up of it into a greater reality, a transformation of the 'earthly' into the 'heavenly' (1 Corinthians

15.42–50). All the evangelists underline their belief that the risen Christ was not a ghost or a spirit, that he truly had a body, even though it was a glorified body. This is weighty testimony.

> Ah! what avails the classic bent
> And what the cultured word
> Against the undoctored incident
> Which actually occurred?[6]

There are many who emphasize the emergence of the Easter Community at Easter. As the disciples gathered after the crucifixion, they experienced the grace and forgiveness of God. Because they had been scattered at the time of the Passion (Mark 14.50 and parallels), their gathering together was itself a kind of grace, a miracle. In this coming together, they found mutual acceptance and forgiveness for having betrayed their Lord.

It is not enough, however, to hold that, somehow, this coming together in itself 'sparked off' belief in the resurrection. The disciples were fearful and mistrustful, even in their coming together (Luke 24.11; John 20.4–10, 19). It was the profound experience of the Risen Lord which made them stay together, and, after Pentecost, to witness together in such a way that they became a world-changing force.[7] Jesus had appeared to them and it is interesting to note how often the evangelists speak of Jesus appearing to them, not a disembodied spirit – not 'the Christ of faith', not even the eternal Logos, just Jesus. 'We see Jesus,' the writer of the Letter to the Hebrews says, and the evangelists agree.

Nor can we be content, as we have seen, only with appearance. It wasn't that this was only a way of appreciating the significance of Jesus for the rest of their lives. It wasn't only that they spoke of the continuing significance of Jesus in the language of apocalyptic and eschatology with which they were familiar. It wasn't just an experience of Jesus as 'present' – analogous to but stronger than the experiences of those who have lost loved ones.

It is significant that the disciples chose the category of 'resurrection' for their discourse. In contemporary Jewish apocalyptic there was, of course, a great deal about resurrection, but it was usually about the General Resurrection; resurrection at the Last Day. There is, however, the somewhat cryptic figure of Enoch who is described as being 'taken up' to God (Genesis 5.24; cf. Hebrews 11.5). Jewish apocalyptic made much of this figure but it is clear that it is the notion of 'ascension' rather than 'resurrection' which is relevant here. Jesus himself, of course, raised individuals from the dead (Mark 5.21–43, Luke 7.11–17, John 11.1–45) but this is, rightly, regarded as resuscitation not resurrection: these individuals were recalled to continue with their natural lives which, presumably, ended in a natural death. Matthew also reports the resurrection of 'the saints' at the time of Jesus' death (27.52–3), though this is more about the anticipation of the fruits of Jesus' death than a statement about the resurrection as such.

There was very little then in the background for the disciples to use for the resurrection of an individual. Indeed, there were other categories they could have used which would not have involved an empty grave. There was the category of 'martyr'. The party of the Zealots used this to celebrate those who had been killed in the cause of resisting the Roman occupation. In doing this, they were continuing a tradition which went back to the Maccabean martyrs of the Seleucid period. It would have been natural for the disciples to have treated Jesus as a righteous martyr whose martyrdom remained significant for the community he had left behind.

Another way in which apocalyptic language was used was that of visions or dreams. Indeed, there are instances of such use in the New Testament itself. If the 'spiritual presence' of Jesus was felt strongly among the disciples, this could have been described in terms of dreams or visions.

It appears that the language of resurrection was used by the disciples because it alone was sufficient to describe what had happened to Jesus. The disciples would have known that this language was developed to describe the collective resurrection at the Last Day. Here, however, was an anticipation of the Last Day! What was happening to Jesus was what they had believed would happen at the *eschaton*. What was it that compelled them to use this language of resurrection? The empty grave would certainly have been one such reason, but another, surely, would have been the nature of the Risen Lord's transformed body. Here was a body that was, in a sense, continuous with the body they had known and yet it was so very different. This was truly how it would be in the Kingdom of Heaven.

It is claimed, sometimes, that the traditions about the empty tomb are late. That the earliest testimonies, Paul's for instance, do not mention it. Where Paul is concerned, he refers repeatedly, directly or indirectly, to Christ's burial and to the close connection between burial and resurrection. As F. F. Bruce has put it, such language 'bespeaks belief in the empty tomb'.[8]

It is indeed remarkable that there was a tomb at all! Criminals executed by crucifixion were not usually accorded the dignity of having a tomb to themselves. At the most, they were thrown into a common pit for executed criminals. This was, presumably, the fate of the two thieves executed along with Jesus (Luke 23.39–43). Jesus was saved from this fate only by the generosity and courage of Joseph of Arimathea.[9] Given, however, that there *was* a tomb, if it had *not* been empty, the easiest thing for the opponents of the Resurrection story would have been to produce the body. Even if the disciples, by some mistake, had gone to the 'wrong' tomb, it would have been easy enough to find the 'right' tomb.

Throughout the centuries, many reasons have been given, by friend and foe alike, for the tomb being empty. One is the so-called 'swoon' theory: it is held that Jesus did not really die on the Cross, he went into a coma. The cool of the tomb revived him, he recovered and escaped! A form of this theory is held, for instance, by *Ahmadiyyah*, a heterodox but very missionary-minded 'Muslim' sect. According to them, after his recovery Jesus went away to Kashmir. There he died a natural death and his real tomb is located in Kashmir (so much for the battle between those who believe the real tomb is located in the Church of the Holy Sepulchre and those who believe it is the Garden Tomb, a little distance away).

Anyone who knows anything about the awful reality of the crucifixion – and the evangelists are remarkably restrained in their accounts – of the dehydration and the bleeding the night before, of the journey to the place of execution, of the body being stretched and broken on the Cross, will know that it is hardly possible for a person to suffer in these ways and then recover so quickly, if at all.

There are some who say that thieves stole the body. Against this, it is often pointed out that grave robbers do not often steal the corpse. They may take what is buried with the body – jewellery, clothes, perfume – but for the body they have little use, especially if it is the broken, mangled body of a crucified man. Then there are others who claim that it was the enemies of Jesus who stole the body. Why should they do so? They knew where he had been buried, and the best plan was to keep a close watch over the tomb to make sure that no one disturbed it. This is precisely what happened according to Matthew (Matthew 27.62–6). Also, if they *had* stolen the body, they could easily have produced it when the story of the Resurrection broke.

The earliest story of all, spread about by the chief priests, was that the disciples themselves had stolen the body (Matthew 28.11–15). This story was still current in the second century when Justin Martyr wrote an account of his *Dialogue with Trypho the Jew*.[10] Indirectly, its continuing currency in the second century suggests that the tomb *was* empty, for whatever reason! This story appears to be the most unconvincing of all. The fearlessness of the disciples after Pentecost compared to their cowardice at the time of the trial and the crucifixion, their readiness to suffer and to be put to death for the sake of the Gospel, is inconsistent with the view that they stole the body.

Why do people find it so difficult to believe in the Resurrection and, particularly, in the empty tomb? It seems that there are various reasons for this attitude which are deeply embedded in a modern, post-enlightenment world view. One has to do with the assumptions of physical determinism which people absorb at school and university (and even in theological colleges). It is taken for granted that the physical universe is a closed system of cause and effect; the one rigidly following the other. Belief in such a universe makes it difficult to give credence to any claim that there can be an intervention which disturbs the causal order of the universe.

Historical study has also been influenced by the determinist paradigm of the physical sciences. An important principle in historical criticism, for example, has been that the new must be evaluated on the basis of the old. There is also an insistence that it is people who must be regarded as the proper subjects of history. God and other 'super-natural' forces are not a proper area for historical study. Both of these positions have been radically criticized by theologians such as Wolfhart Pannenberg in Germany and Jon Sobrino, a Latin American liberation theologian. Both hold that the history of Jesus is important for faith and we cannot deal with the significant events of Jesus' life without a reassessment of historical methods. If we are to take the biblical material seriously, we must deal with what was 'new' in Jesus without constantly trying to explain it in terms of the old. Even if we cannot grasp all that is new about the Risen Christ, we can still study and evaluate the *events* which disclosed this 'newness', however patchily and sporadically, in the present order. Historical method should be able to consider the possibility of divine intervention. That is to say, it should be possible for *God* to be the subject of history and not only human beings.[11]

Where physical determinism is concerned, our own experience of freedom is a standing contradiction of it. We continually intervene in the natural order to fulfil the purposes and goals we have established for ourselves and which, we believe, have not been previously determined by physical processes. On the contrary, we believe that our purposes and goals determine the physicality around us. Humanity is thus not only a product of the physical and living universe, it also has the capacity to bring profound changes to its environment and, indeed, to the world at large.[12]

The question, of course, is whether we can deny to the Supreme Being an indefinitely greater measure of the freedom to intervene in the universe than we experience ourselves in increasingly remarkable ways?

Another kind of objection to the resurrection story (and, indeed, *a fortiori*, to any kind of divine intervention) is the moral one. It is asked, for instance, why, if God could rescue the Hebrews from Egypt and then from drowning in the Red Sea, did he not save the Jews from Nazi concentration camps? This is the objection of those who reject what they call 'laser-beam' type miracles. Such an objection is often based, however, on a misunderstanding of God's nature: God is not like Superman and the history of his saving acts is not like a series of Superman films! It may also be based on a misunderstanding of the nature of the universe in which we live. If God has created a universe with definite laws and order but in other respects free to develop in its own way, then we should expect things to go 'wrong' from time to time. If, for other reasons, we believe that God is love then clearly this is the best of all possible worlds, but it is not perfect in the sense a mechanism might be perfect. It is an evolving world in which there is waste and suffering. In such a world, God is graciously present and working out his purposes but in these he can be resisted not only by rebellious humanity but also by the 'obstructiveness' of nature. There is a struggle going on between good and evil, God and the devil, the world of the spirit and the

68

world of the 'flesh': the Hebrews were slaves in Egypt for many years before God could rescue them.

Signs of the struggle are all around us but there are also many signs that the good is triumphing over evil. Every act of love, of courage and sacrifice, of generosity and hospitality is a sign of God's goodness. So are the beauties of nature, the fruitfulness of the earth, the wonderful checks and balances which provide order in the cosmos and make life and thought possible. There are what we may term 'natural' signs. God also gives us 'special signs' of his presence and love. He reveals his will through the prophets and his love in events which save people from disease or war or famine. The resurrection of Jesus Christ from the dead shows us not only the profundity of the struggle but also the glorious destiny which God has for us. We are, after all, not just bits of bio-chemistry. We have an awareness of our spiritual nature and its destiny. The resurrection shows us that the whole of our person shares in our destiny. We are not merely spiritual beings, we are also embodied beings and our bodies too need to be transformed if we are to experience the wholeness of resurrection.

The Resurrection of Christ is, of course, the definitive sign for us of God's gracious presence and purposes. Even in the course of Jesus' ministry, however, there were other signs which revealed God's work to the percipient. According to C. K. Barrett, in St John's Gospel signs are 'special demonstrations of the character and power of God, and partial but effective realizations of his salvation'.[13]

In his graciousness, God continues to provide such signs both in and beyond the Church. Wherever people are healed, physically, emotionally and spiritually; wherever there is reconciliation and peace; wherever communities and families are made whole; God's presence and work may be seen. The life of Jesus, his death and his Resurrection provide us with the perspectives which make recognition of this divine presence possible.

Bishop Hassan Dehqani Tafti, formerly Bishop in Iran, and the whole Church in Iran suffered grievously both during and after the so-called Islamic revolution in that country. He has written a beautiful Easter Hymn in Persian which recalls St Athanasius' words that Christians who suffer are able to do so because of the sure and certain hope which they have in the resurrection of Christ.[14] Here is a translation of a part of the hymn:

Spread the news! Look abroad
He has risen to reign!
Now at last heaven is open'd
to earth once again
Now that death's power is spent
and is vanquished for aye,
Who should fear any storm,
who now cringe in dismay?
Lift your eyes to the hills,
greet the bright rising sun;
Now our hearts and our souls
are renewed all as one!
See, the tomb is found bare;
this the work of God's hand;
See our Jesus now risen,
In this faith may we stand![5]

Christ Will Come Again!

Remembering what God has done in the past strengthens us to live in the present and gives us hope for the future. This view of God's providence has led the Judaeo-Christian tradition to develop a view of history which is at once unified and sees significance in the particular histories of peoples and nations. Such a view also has a 'forward' thrust to it: God is working out his purposes and both humanity and the rest of creation have destinies towards which they are moving. In other traditions we find narrative and legend and, among the Greeks and Romans, histories of particular periods or campaigns, such as the Persian or Peloponnesian Wars, but there is little sense of a universal history moving towards a meaningful end. Islam, of course, in this sense, stands alongside the Judaeo-Christian tradition. A judicial interest in precedents set by the Prophet of Islam led to the development of the science of Sunnah, and historians such as Al-Tabari and Ibn Khaldun developed overviews of world history and related them to revelation.

Folk religious traditions differ widely among themselves, of course, but they often have a cyclical view of history where progress is followed by regress and every end with going back to the beginning. In some cases, the dead may go to a world of spirits but they can return from there and, in any case, there is no concept of judgement or salvation based on moral considerations.

It is important, at this stage, to stress that native European traditions, such as the Scandinavian or Celtic, do not have a sense of history of the kind referred to above. The importance of historical understanding in Europe has come about because of the influence of the Judaeo-Christian tradition. The decline of Marxism as an alternative interpretation of history, and the emergence of neo-paganisms of various kinds may again result in a situation where history is no longer regarded as important.

Cultures formed by the Indic tradition (and in this respect Hinduism and Buddhism are similar) also tend to have a cyclical view of time. Fulfilment is seen here not as the climax of time but as an *escape* from its cyclical nature in which all existent beings are trapped. The late Bishop Lakshman Wickremesinghe of Sri Lanka used to point out that the emergence of Salvation History as a paradigm in biblical theology has obscured for Christians other ways of reading the Bible. For instance, it has relegated to the background rich material having to do with God's presence in creation. Similarly, it has obscured the illumination of human hearts and minds by the divine Logos and the work of the Holy Spirit in creation, in societies and in the lives of individuals. The Salvation History approach has made us read the Bible like a history book. But the Bible is much more than that. It also contains poetry, wisdom and romance. All of these can lead to an encounter with the divine.

6

Christ Will Come Again:
Salvation and Judgement

*

The Bible provides an overall framework for understanding the human condition and, indeed, the world as a whole, which has to do with God's purposes, how they are thwarted or fulfilled and the final triumph of God's will and of those who seek to live according to it. This view is rooted in the 'this-worldly' attitude of the early Hebrews who thought of achievement and prosperity in this life for both individual and community. It is not surprising, therefore, that the earliest reflections on the future in the Bible have to do with the destiny of Israel itself.

Such a destiny is seen in different ways. It is seen as a vanquishing of her enemies or as her former enemies coming to Mount Zion to pay tribute to her God or as a state of peace between Israel and her neighbours. Gradually, however, the question of judgement comes to the fore. At first, this is judgement of Israel's oppressors but eventually it is of Israel herself, her rulers and priests. The emergence of this self-critical principle in the Bible is of huge importance in a world full of self-confident chauvinism.

One of the distinctive elements in Old Testament prophecy is the ability of the prophets to criticize their own people and to refuse to be oracles who merely confirm their people's prejudices. The Day of the Lord emerges out of these ideas of judgement and salvation for Israel and her neighbours. At first, it is seen in temporal terms; as a day in the future when God will judge Israel and her neighbours or, alternatively, a day when God will save Israel from her neighbours or even with her neighbours.

It is only in the comparatively late books of the Hebrew Testament that we get a full blown eschatology which looks forward to the end of chronological time itself and to the judgement of the whole human race after a general resurrection from the dead. Such language is to be found, for example, in the Book of Daniel. This remarkable book not only uses both Hebrew and Aramaic but has a large number of Persian loan words.[1] It uses apocalyptic idiom to describe God's ultimate triumph over evil and the imagery here and elsewhere in the Bible may well be influenced by Zoroastrianism.[2]

Jesus and the Kingdom

By the time of the New Testament, this idiom had become firmly rooted in Jewish thought and it is not a surprise, therefore, to find it being used in the New Testament itself. It is widely recognized that the future orientation of much prophetic activity is highlighted in apocalyptic literature. The New Testament also has this orientation towards the future but, crucially, there is also tension between the present and the future which gives much of the New Testament its distinctive character. C. K. Barrett has pointed out that this tension is signalled, for example, in St John's Gospel in phrases such as 'the hour comes and now is' (4.23; 5.25).[3] There is a tension between the realization that the Kingdom of God is imminent – this is the burden of the teaching of the Synoptic Jesus – and the realization by the Church that the Kingdom is present in Jesus himself. 'The Kingdom of God is in your midst' (Luke 17.21). Moltmann, commenting on Schweitzer's remark that Jesus preached the Kingdom and the Church preached Jesus, points out that this was because the Church realized that the Kingdom was already present in Jesus. It was not a category mistake but an awareness that the one who preached the Kingdom with such urgency was the first fruits of his own preaching![4] Jesus is truly *autobasileia*, himself the Kingdom.

While there is a lively expectation in the New Testament of the fulfilment of the Kingdom which has been inaugurated in the preaching, teaching, living, dying and rising of Jesus, there is also a measure of caution. Even in the earliest books, such as the Letters to the Thessalonians, there is caution about speculation regarding the *parousia* or Coming of the Lord. It is interesting, in this connection, to observe that the resources for dealing with the delay of the Lord's return are already present in the early material.

Without such resources, early Christianity would rapidly have become another messianic sect and would have ceased to be credible. This combination of expectation and caution continued for some time in the early period of Christian history. 'Expectation' was often characteristic of groups which were not at the centre of the Church's affairs, such as the Montanists of Asia and North Africa.

Gradually, however, the focus of interest shifted from an expectation of the Lord's personal return in glory to other ways of experiencing his presence and other ways of thinking about the future. Even so, it has never died away altogether, surviving in liturgy and in popular devotion in a quite remarkable way. From time to time, there are 'revivals' in which 'expectation' of the Lord and of his Kingdom are, once again, central features.

The Lord in the Church

There seem to have been three main reasons for this shift in focus and emphasis. First, there was the emergence of a truly realized eschatology which emphasized the presence of Jesus in the Church. Jesus was present in the apostolic preaching. It is interesting that in 'the Great Commission' the promise of the Lord's presence goes hand in hand with the missionary mandate (Matthew 28.19, 20)[5] The same Gospel teaches that the Lord is present where two or three are gathered in his name (Matthew 18.20) and the teaching of virtually the whole of the New Testament is that Jesus is present in the Church through the Holy Spirit (see, for example, the farewell discourses in St John's Gospel chapters 14—16). It is in the sacraments of baptism and eucharist, however, that the Lord's presence is, perhaps, most tangible for the believer and for the Church. In baptism the believer experiences a dying and a rising in the Lord (e.g. Romans 6.1–11) and in the bread and wine of the eucharist there is an experience of the Lord's presence, especially in terms of partaking of the benefits of his sacrifice and of communion in his suffering (John 6; 1 Corinthians 10.16–21; 11.23–34, Hebrews 13.10–15).

Secondly, there was an increasing concern with the afterlife, with what happens after death, and elaborations of what is supposed to occur. Now it is true that the Bible teaches some kind of survival after death. This may be seen as God reclaiming the breath of life (Psalm 104.29; Ecclesiastes 12.7), as a rest from the labours of this life (Revelation 14.13), as entrusting our spirits into God's keeping (Luke 23.46; Acts 7.59), or as the believer's departure from this life (Luke 2.29; 2 Timothy 4.6; 2 Peter 1.15). Believers may be confident that they will come into the presence of the Lord (2 Corinthians 5.8; Philippians 1.23). At the same time it has to be said that the characteristic teaching of the Bible and of both Jewish and Christian tradition is that of the resurrection of the dead, which is seen as the reconstitution of the whole personality. Setting aside some crudely materialistic views which have had currency in both traditions, this comes down to belief in some kind of embodied existence which is both continuous with the past and different from it. For Christians, the risen Christ is the pattern for reflection on what resurrection might mean for us (1 Corinthians 15.20–57). Gradually, however, under the influence of Platonists, there was a shift of interest from 'resurrection of the body' to the 'immortality of the soul'. The focus was now not so much on God's gracious act in raising us to share in the risen life of his Son but on the essential nature of the soul as incapable of dissolution – and on what happens to it after physical death. The emphasis, then, came to be on our spiritual destiny beyond this life and not on the End when Christ will gather all things to himself in a renewed creation (Ephesians 1.10; Revelation 21.5).

The Kingdom and the State

Thirdly, attention was detracted from the *parousia* because of the increasing identification of the Byzantine state with the Kingdom of God on earth.[6] Such a close identification was always open to challenge by theologians. St Augustine, for instance, has provided us with the distinction between the *civitas terrena*, the earthly city established by God to promote justice and good order, and the *civitas Dei*, the city of God, consisting of those who have been reborn of God's grace. Although Augustine himself acknowledged the 'mixed' nature of the Church, and believed that it would be purified only at the Day of Judgement and was willing to recognize 'signs' of the Kingdom outside the Church, there was a later tendency in the Western Church to identify the Kingdom of God with the Church. It is true, of course, that the Church manifests the Kingdom and has been entrusted with its keys (Matthew 16.19;

18.18; John 20.22–3). It is true that the Church has been commissioned to preach the Gospel, the good news of the Kingdom, not only to the whole of humanity but to the whole of creation and even to the principalities and powers in the heavenly places (Matthew 28.19, 20; Mark 16.15; Ephesians 3.10). The scope of the Kingdom is, nevertheless, much wider than just the Church. It has to do with nothing less than the renewal of the whole of creation. The Church's witness has a role in this but, in the end, it is to come about through God's intervention in bringing the whole story of creation and redemption to a climax. The Kingdom is then to be seen as revealed in Jesus, manifest in the Church's witness, worship and work, but also awaited as the 'Kingdom of glory', to be brought about by divine initiative.

Millenarianism and its Rejection

From time to time, moreover, there have been movements of protests against an over-identification of the Kingdom with the Church or the State. Millenarianism is an umbrella term used to describe ideas and movements of different kinds. In its pre-millennial form it is found at different periods in the history of the Church. Typically, its adherents hold that Christ will return personally to inaugurate a millennial reign on earth before the last judgement and the ushering in of the Kingdom. Pre-millennialism emphasizes the discontinuity between the present order and the inauguration of a millennial order. There have been important revivals, based on readings of the book of Revelation in the Bible, in the seventeenth century and early in the nineteenth century. These revivals have had very important social, political and theological consequences. They have, for instance, given rise to Christian Zionism, to the view that the Jewish people must return to the Holy Land before Christ came to reign for a thousand years. Such a view had only a slender basis in traditional Christian exegesis before the rise of these movements. The nearest, perhaps, is in the writings of some of the Puritans who believed that the Jews would return to their land, but only after they had been converted! Many Christian societies with a concern for the Jewish people have their roots in these revivals.

Although the Church was certainly not identified with the Kingdom, there was, nevertheless, a concern for the Church's purity in readiness for the coming of Christ, the bridegroom. This led to the emergence of 'holiness' movements and to sectarian and semi-sectarian tendencies. The nineteenth century revival took place within the Evangelical movement and was, to some extent, related to the Evangelical revival as a whole. Through the Irvingites and others, it had an impact, nevertheless, that went far beyond this constituency. Many mainstream Evangelicals, on the other hand, were cautious and even suspicious of the movements. Charles Simeon, for example, wrote at the time that he was much more concerned that people should come to a personal experience of faith in Christ and the salvation this brings than in the minutiae of millenarian expectation! Similarly, Thomas Scott, the first Secretary of the Church Missionary Society, believed that the Kingdom would not be inaugurated by a sudden return of Christ to earth but by the gradual accumulation of 'signs' which occurred at critical junctures in human history. In this sense, Scott was much more of a post-millennialist and had affinities with certain kinds of liberal thought which tended to identify the Kingdom with human material, social and moral progress. As we shall see, there have been more recent exponents of such ideas, but there have also been severe critics, particularly in the light of the two world wars and numerous other conflicts which this century has spawned.[7]

There were others, however, who rejected pre-millennial views for very different reasons. Many were coming to realize that the time scale of the universe, produced by Bishop Ussher, was not at all adequate, that the world had existed for very much longer than Ussher had imagined and that it could be expected to last for much longer than pre-millennialists wanted it to last! Those with such views of the universe also often saw it as a closed system of cause and effect, gradually moving to entropy where heat was uniformly distributed and was not, therefore, available for work. Such a state could be described as the heat death of the universe.

With such a view of the universe, how can one speak of the Kingdom of God? Those who tended to accept such a view of the fate of the physical universe, emphasized the transcendent nature of the human self whose destiny could not be defined by the physical universe. They also emphasized the destiny of human society as its moral perfection, its fundamental difference from the animal world and its capacity to approach the divine. Many of them could not resist the temptation of seeing at least the reflection of such a society in the nineteenth century European state!

Such ideas had considerable influence in the development of the liberal consensus and it was only in the closing years of the nineteenth century and the early years of the twentieth century that they began to be challenged.[8] They were challenged because the apprehension of the approaching European catastrophe, which culminated in World War I, made belief in steady-state progress impossible. Both Johannes Weiss (1863–1914) and Albert Schweitzer (1875–1965) felt that the story of Jesus had been cast too much in the mould of nineteenth century European liberalism. They wished to emphasize, instead, the apocalyptic background and colouring of Jesus' preaching: he had expected the Kingdom to come quickly and had tried to accelerate its arrival by sacrificing himself. The Kingdom had not come and Jesus had died a failure. The purpose of such writing was not to underline the failure of Jesus' ministry but to point out how alien were the categories in which Jesus and the early Church thought from those in which modern Western Europeans were beginning to think. Such a view of Jesus' 'failure' sometimes has strange results. Mark Tully, in his BBC series entitled *The Lives of Jesus*, comes to a similar conclusion but, somewhat paradoxically, this leads him to a belief in the truth of the Resurrection! A 'failed' Jesus could not have kick-started the Church into existence and a dramatic event, such as the Resurrection, is required to account for the Church.

Weiss and Schweitzer, themselves, could only try and rescue an effective teacher of ethical truths from the wreckage of New Testament studies which they had created, but their work put paid to the liberal Protestant Jesus who was seen as a kind of enlightened statesman whose ideas could be the basis for the development of a liberal society which could approximate more and more to the Kingdom of God which he had heralded!

Jesus and History

Theologians such as Wolfhart Pannenberg and Jürgen Moltmann have, more recently, tried to rescue eschatology from such a negative judgement. The result of this judgement was the emergence of a host of theologies which emphasized the existential over the historical. If very little could be known about the historical

Jesus, and if what *could* be known was almost incomprehensible to us, then *my* experience of the Risen Christ in the Church, the Sacraments or in preaching became primary. Such a 'Christ of faith' is very plastic indeed and can be moulded to fit an indefinite number of situations. That is its attraction but is also its danger.

While fully recognizing the historically conditioned character of eschatological language in the Bible, theologians such as Moltmann and Pannenberg have identified the category of future hope as of continuing significance for us. They have challenged deterministic views of history and have maintained that history has to do with the *novum*, with what is new and which cannot be fitted into schemes which are either physically or spiritually deterministic. They have emphasized the importance of God's agency for history. It may well be that the *totality* of an act of God cannot be comprehended by the historians, but they must take account of the *difference* such an act has made in the world and in the lives of men and women. This is particularly true of the resurrection of Jesus Christ from the dead. It is true, as Pannenberg says, that the resurrection is not simply one event among others. It has cosmic significance and is nothing less than the beginning of a new creation. Its impact on the disciples, however, is open to historical investigation as are other aspects of the resurrection such as the empty tomb.

For Moltmann, the central teaching of Scripture, seen most clearly in accounts of the resurrection of Jesus Christ from the dead, is God's purpose for the redemption of the whole created order. Both Moltmann and Pannenberg emphasize the proleptic nature of Christ's resurrection: it is God's future with us and that is why it both changes and shapes the course of history.[9]

Views of the resurrection as the coming of God's future to us and as determining the course of history have been important influences on the work of liberation theologians in Latin America and elsewhere. Theologians, such as Jon Sobrino, have argued that the resurrection is hope in the face of hopelessness and that it inspires the struggle of the oppressed against poverty, tyranny and injustice. Those who are involved in such a struggle are inspired by the Cross and understand the sacrificial nature of their calling. They are able to do this because they know the future has already been revealed in the resurrection. God is himself striving to bring about the renewal of all creation so that it conforms to what has been given in the resurrection.[10]

Contrary to the widespread misunderstanding of their work, such theologians are also very concerned about the *inner* transformation of the individual in conformity with the pattern given in the resurrection but this is set in the context of social transformation, with the movement of society towards conformity with the Kingdom of God as revealed in the resurrection. There is a mutuality between the individual and social aspects of transformation. The individual certainly generates the movement for the social but, it can also be said, the social makes individual transformation possible. Liberation theologians often speak of those struggling for the Kingdom as being fellow-workers with God (1 Corinthians 3.9; 2 Corinthians 6.1). This does not at all mean that the Kingdom can be brought about by human endeavour alone. It is true that human beings witness to the Kingdom and contribute to it in a small way. In the end, however, the Kingdom is completed and fulfilled by divine intervention itself.

Fulfilment in Christ

Apart from liberation theology, there have been other attempts to speak of the coming of God's Kingdom. Once again, these have been based on an open view of the universe and on the possibility of God's activity in it. One such attempt is that of the French Jesuit, Teilhard de Chardin. Teilhard was a palaeontologist who spent much of his working life in China. From the 1920s his ideas on evolution and its relation to sin had led to the prohibition on teaching which was maintained for the rest of his life. As a scientist, Teilhard was well aware of the increasing complexification of life, as it is observed in biological evolution. For him, evolution is an ascent towards consciousness, which is supremely manifested in humanity.

Human society, however, also manifests this complexification. In fact, humanity is the link between the living world and God – and part of its responsibility is to bring about the fulfilment of the Cosmos, as everything converges to the supreme centre, *Omega*. Teilhard's system is reminiscent of the 'Irenaean' stream of Christian theological tradition which emphasizes *anakephalaiosis* or recapitulation, the fulfilment of all things in Christ. For Teilhard too, the evolution and complexification of human society is seen as leading to the *pleroma*, a term he uses again and again. It is leading towards the fulfilment of God's purposes for the universe. In some ways Teilhard is a panentheist. He thinks of God, and even of Christ, as immanent in the world (he speaks, for instance, of the Cosmos being Christ's body). At the same time, he can speak of the world as coming to its fullest expression in Christ.

Teilhard has been criticized for a kind of facile optimism in suggesting that social and even technological complexification will, in themselves, lead towards the Kingdom of God. They may not at all. They may have a tendency towards quite another sort of Kingdom! It is here that protagonists for Teilhard and those for liberation theology are in vigorous dialogue with each other. Teilhard's system appears to exclude the direct intervention, revolutionary struggle and dramatic change which the liberation theologians are discussing. His system has more to do with accumulation, aggregation and culmination.[11]

'The End of History'

After the end of the Cold War, historians, such as Francis Fukuyama of the US State Department, began to talk about the 'end of history': now that conflict between the superpowers had ceased, the future could only be understood in terms of the triumph of capitalism and of the democracy it is alleged to promote.[12] President George Bush, on the other hand, in a speech to the General Assembly of the United Nations, spoke of 'the renewal of history'. On the face of it, this is a hopeful expression, but a closer reading shows that Bush is, in fact, arguing for a continuing role for the United States in the policing of the world because of continuing and renewed regional and local conflict.

Samuel Huntington of Princeton has written about 'the clash of civilizations'. He has identified a number of civilizations such as the Islamic, Confucian, Slavonic, Western etc. These are based on shared religious, cultural and political assumptions. Huntington's thesis is that the interests of these civilizations are bound to be in conflict and this could result in another kind of cold war among them or even armed hostilities. Naturally, in such a situation, the West will have to look to its own interests.[13]

It is obvious from the above that history is often understood to be the history of *conflict*, whether that is between the superpowers, various civilizations or nations or even *within* nations. From the

Christian point of view, this is a somewhat negative view. Christians acknowledge the dangers of actual or potential conflict. Indeed, as Hans Küng has rightly pointed out, there will be no peace in the world unless there is peace between peoples and nations and there will be no peace between the nations unless there is peace between the religions. To this we might add that there will be no peace *within* nations unless there is peace between the religions.[14]

History is not, however, just about conflict. It is also about cooperation. Many of Huntington's civilizations would not have existed if people of *different* faiths, languages and cultures had not cooperated. This is true, for example, of the so-called 'Islamic Civilization'. Not only have people of diverse ethnic and cultural backgrounds contributed to it; the role of Christians and Jews has been formative in the areas of spirituality, philosophy, science, jurisprudence and even architecture.[15] History is, moreover, about achievement and failure. It is about relationships between people; whether there are nation states, local communities, families or communities of faith.

Not even the coming of the Kingdom of God, let alone the cessation of a Cold War, can mean the end of history. The French mystic François de Sales has said, 'after the journey to God, there is the journey in God'. This may be the present experience of mystics but it is also the future of all human beings. Our development does not cease when we draw near to God and God to us.[16] As Moltmann has put it, we continue to become the persons God wants us to be for the sake of his Kingdom.[17]

The Scope of the Kingdom

The scope of God's Kingdom is not, of course, just Israel or the Church, it is not even the whole of humanity. It is nothing less than the whole of creation. This theme develops gradually and variously throughout the Bible but it is deeply rooted in the biblical insight that the God who has revealed himself to the People of Israel is the God and Creator of the whole universe; of all the worlds and of all humanity. As such, God has a purpose for each human being and for the whole of creation. This is the basis of a truly biblical universalism and it is in sharp contrast to the narrowly parochial and tribal religion of most of Israel's neighbours.

It is true that Israel did not always recognize the implications of its own faith, just as the Church has not. It was believed sometimes that the 'witness' of Israel to the nations was to bring God's judgement upon them for their oppression of Israel, their idolatries, their superstitions and their tyrannies. There is, of course, some truth in this view but it is not the whole story as the Servant Songs make clear. The Servant not only brings 'judgement' to the nations but also 'salvation' (Isaiah 42.1–4; cf. 49.1–6).[18] Underlying the biblical material there is a sense of this universal concern. Again, it is true that Israel sometimes believed that God's universal purposes would be fulfilled by making everyone like them! The visions in Isaiah and Micah can be read in this way (Isaiah 2.1–4; Micah 4.1–4). Such a centripetal view of mission is not, of course, limited to ancient Israel. This kind of 'judaizing' tendency is often present in the way we think about and practise mission today: let us make everyone exactly like ourselves! Mission in these cases is not so much about proclaiming and living the Kingdom as the transference of cultural values.[19]

It is the Prophets who realized that God's universal concern was not about making everyone a 'Zionist'. God was active among the nations *as they were* and his work among them was not utterly unlike his work in Israel. In a key passage in the book of Amos, God tells the Israelites that just as he had brought the Israelites out of Egypt, so he had been working among the Ethiopians, the Syrians and the Philistines (Amos 9.7–8). It is interesting to note that the list contains names of both traditional enemies of Israel as well as of people who were regarded as 'far away'. The distinguished Waldensian commentator, Alberto Soggin, has this to say: 'So the other nations also have a history of salvation, even if they are unaware of it and Israel does not recognize it: their migrations too, are to be seen in the context of the saving plan of God.'[20] In the same way, the Prophet Malachi, while criticizing Israel's faithlessness, tells us that God's name is honoured among the nations (Malachi 1.11). Some Bible translations attempt to resolve the difficulty of this verse by making the sense of it future. In the early Church, similarly, it was believed that this was a looking forward to the universal celebration of the Eucharist. Pious as these thoughts are, there does not appear to be any futurity in this verse. The sense, rather, seems to be that even the gentiles, who know God only through creation and conscience, can honour him when his chosen people, even with their revelation, have turned away from him.

God's universal purposes are surely being worked out and their fulfilment will be revealed at the climax of world history: 'In that day Israel will be the third with Egypt and Assyria, a blessing in the midst of the earth, whom the LORD of hosts has blessed, saying, "Blessed be Egypt my people, and Assyria the work of my hands, and Israel my heritage" ' (Isaiah 19.24).

Jesus was quick to perceive that the response to his ministry came from the poor, the foreigners and the socially marginalized. It is this which lies behind the universal vision of the New Testament. It is not that the early Christian missionaries went to the gentiles because their preaching had been rejected in the synagogues. The universalist dynamic of Christian mission is, rather, deeply rooted in the biblical view of God and in the experience of Jesus himself.

We have seen then that the scope of God's redeeming work is universal because the scope of his creating work is universal. God is working out his purposes not only in every people and culture but throughout creation. How can we discern where God is working in the history of a particular people? It is here that the Salvation History which we find in the Bible is helpful. Such a Salvation History does not mean that there are no other 'salvation histories', on the contrary, biblical Salvation History enables us to discover 'salvation histories' in other cultures and peoples: if this is the way in which God has worked in Israel, in Jesus and in the Church, how may we expect him to be working in this culture or that people? Such a 'salvation history' cannot always be equated with the *religious* history of a people. It may be that organized and institutionalized religion has been experienced not as salvation but as oppressive and exploitative. Sometimes salvation history may be seen in 'counter-religious' movements. In the Indian context, for example, the rigid caste system of Vedic Hinduism has been challenged, from time to time, by radical movements such as Buddhism, Sikhism, Sufism and even Christianity! Is God seen to be preparing people for revelation in the caste-bound aspects of Hinduism or in these, and other, movements of revival, renewal and challenge? There may have to be a negation of false religion before there is an affirmation of authentic religion.

God's purposes for humanity are definitively disclosed in Christ and the 'salvation histories' of the various peoples are leading to fulfilment in Christ, though not necessarily in historic, institutional Christianity. If, however, the key to a final understanding of any salvation history is Christ himself, then it becomes more, not less urgent to preach the Gospel. This should not mean trying to make people like ourselves. This Gospel has to be made intelligible to people in terms of their own world view and spiritual idiom. Indeed, this is the *only way* in which it can be made intelligible.

What then is the fate of those who die without realizing or acknowledging that Christ is the key to their personal or communal destiny? We must be clear that people cannot be saved by the practice of their religion alone (however good that is) nor by their upstanding morality (however admirable that may be). The witness of the Bible, as a whole, is that people are saved by God's gracious and merciful initiative and not because they deserve to be or because of anything they have done. The universalism of both the Hebrew Bible and of the New Testament has shown us, moreover, that God's gracious purpose is for all: God is the Saviour of all (1 Timothy 4.10) and he is uniting all things in Christ (Ephesians 1.10). But what is at the human end of such undeserved grace? It is certainly not self-confidence and pride in one's morality or religious practice. It must be a sense of brokenness and of inadequacy before God, leading to repentance and dependence on God's mercy. The spiritual literatures of many religions and cultures are full of accounts of people who have experienced such a brokenness and dependence on God. Dare we deny that this is a result of the Holy Spirit's work in their lives? We trust in God's mercy for them as we do for ourselves.

It has to be said, however, that God's universal purposes need to be held in tension with the real freedom which human beings have been given. Freedom is a quality we not only experience directly ourselves but we also impute it to others. The notion that we are free to make moral and spiritual decisions is at the heart of every human culture. As the famous Sufi Maulana Rumi has said:

> Does any wise or reasonable person give commands to marble?
> Does he show anger and enmity at bricks and stones?[1]

If human beings are truly free they must be free to reject as well as to accept God's salvation. Could they continue to reject such a salvation for all eternity? Some believe that God's love is so strong that, in the end, it will overcome even the most obdurate sinner.

Let us hope and pray that is the case. In the meanwhile, we have seen the fullest expression of this love in the weakness of the Cross, where it invites but does not coerce. There are others who believe that those who continue in rebellion against God will simply be annihilated. They will cease to exist. This view seems not to take seriously enough the biblical anthropology that men and women have been made in the image of God and, through the breathing-in of God's Spirit, have come to be in an eternal relationship with God. It also, perhaps, does not take into account the judgement we experience because of our continuing state of rebellion. To many it has seemed an easy way out of the dilemma.[22]

In his commentary on St Paul's Letter to the Romans, *Wrestling with Romans*, Bishop John Robinson has pointed out that God is only love. Those who respond to God's love, experience it as love, while those who reject it, experience that same love as God's wrath. God has a purpose for all – he wants to save all. If some are found to have been rejected after all, that is because *they* have rejected God. In the plan of salvation, there is no coercion, only loving invitation. Our destiny depends on how we respond to such a loving invitation, however we come to experience it.[23]

The Coming of the Messiah

The messianic idea emerges in the Bible from a sense of history and its purposiveness and the related notion of End or climax. On the one hand, there is the recognition that God has created the world and humanity and that Israel has been chosen to be a particular vehicle of the divine will. On the other, there is a profound awareness that things have gone wrong in a radical way; that even in Israel there is rebellion, blindness and unfaithfulness.

There is a desire for restoration, for return, for the inauguration of a perfect society where all can flourish and where there is peace: peace between Israel and her neighbours and peace within Israel. There is also an expectation of peace in the wider sense; the restoration of harmony in the created order – the wolf dwelling with the lamb, the leopard lying down with the kid and the suckling child playing over the hole of an asp (Isaiah 11.6–9). The coming of the Messiah is seen as inaugurating such an age of peace and prosperity.

The messianic idea also develops in relation to Israel's sense of holiness as the Chosen People of God. The messianic figure is seen as the priest who makes things right with God (Psalm 110.4; Hebrews 8). Then there is the Messiah as prophet. In the book of Deuteronomy, Moses reminds the people that God 'will raise up a prophet like me from among you' (Deuteronomy 18.15). Modern critical study of the Bible is divided about whether a *particular* prophet is intended or whether this passage deals with prophets generically, since it goes on to discuss the distinguishing of genuine prophets from false ones (verses 21–2). Whatever the sense of this specific passage, the prophetic aspect of the Messiah's work has come to be important for both Jews and Christians (and, indeed, Muslims). This is partly because this recalls the critical principle in the Judaeo-Christian tradition. The Bible is unique, among the world's various scriptures, in having a principle within it which allows a radical criticism of the cult and the law which are part of the prophet's *own* tradition.

The Messiah is also, of course, seen as *King*; the one who inaugurates God's kingdom of righteousness and peace. The *malekut shamayim* (literally the Kingdom of Heaven) is an expression which has its origins in Jewish expectations of the future. Here God is seen as intervening decisively on behalf of his people and liberating them from the clutches of the enemy. The coming of the Messiah is the beginning of God's just reign.

In Jewish thought, the Messiah is certainly a figure for the future. This came about partly because of the recurrent disappointments the Jewish people here had to endure. It also came about because many were thought to be the Messiah and turned out not to be. Thought of as future, the Messiah is a guarantor that God is, after all, faithful in his purposes and promises. Whatever the present may be like, God will show us at the end that he has been in control of history throughout.

A future orientation is also given by the fact that the messianic nature of some individuals and communities has been, at the same time, both authentic and unfulfilled. Moses, for instance, is a messianic figure. The Exodus is a messianic event, perhaps the archetypal messianic event. The figures of David and of his descendants are, perhaps, most closely associated with the Messiah. Indeed, Israel as a whole, or a faithful remnant within it, can be spoken of in this way. At the same time, it is clear that the idea is not completely fulfilled in any of these figures.

Christians, of course, identify the messianic figure with Jesus of Nazareth. Of course, to say that the messianic idea is manifested in Jesus, even defined in Jesus, is not to say that it is fulfilled, in every respect, in the historical Jesus. It is obvious from the New Testament that, in certain respects, the messianic idea has not yet been fulfilled. This is why Christians look forward to the *parousia* when Israel will be vindicated, the reign of God ushered in and the Kingdom delivered to the Father. Jesus has *inaugurated* the Kingdom and he will be revealed as the Messiah in all his glory when the Kingdom is consummated.

There is then a real affinity between the Jewish and Christian experiences in terms of 'already' and 'not yet'. Christians see the contours of the Messiah to come in terms of Jesus of Nazareth. Jews may see it in some other way. It remains true, however, that both are expecting the Messiah to come in glory so that God's purposes may be fulfilled. Surely, this can be an element in Jewish–Christian dialogue?[24]

7

The Ground of Our Meeting

✳

In the Hebrew Bible, the first reference to the Spirit of God is in terms of the 'divine storm' which stirs up the sea of nothingness as a prelude to the Creation. Although Gerhard Von Rad recognizes this role of the Spirit at the very beginning of creation, he then goes on to say that, as far as the Old Testament is concerned, the Spirit 'takes no more active part in creation'. This is surprising, for in Psalm 33, Luther notwithstanding, there is a reference precisely to the cosmological role of the Spirit in creation which Von Rad denies. Such a role is alongside that of the Word and complements it: the Spirit is the vital breath of God which receives creative form from his Word. Also, in the composite Yahwistic-Priestly material of Chapter two of the Book of Genesis, Von Rad himself points out that Adam becomes human only when inspired by the divine breath of life.[1]

The Word and the Spirit

It is important not to distinguish too sharply the different aspects of God's creative activity and, especially, not to assign different spheres of activity to the Word and the Spirit. It may be, however, that the Word and the Spirit focus for us specific dimensions of God's creative work. If, for instance, the Word, or the Logos, is about the order of creation then the Spirit may be about its wonder. Science has long emphasized the lawfulness or orderliness of creation but is now increasingly waking up to its mystery and wonder. Many scientists have been believers because they have felt that the orderliness of creation needed an explanation. Others have felt, however, that religion and science are closest at this point of

wonder and awe at the simplicity of creation and yet its infinite
variety.

The early Christians often thought of the Word as the 'reason'
or the 'harmony' of the universe.[2] If this is so, the Spirit can
perhaps be thought of as the 'power' or the 'energy', which
sustains creation and moves it forward.[3] Again, the Word of God,
incarnate in Jesus of Nazareth, is called the light which enlightens
all (John 1.9), while the Holy Spirit may be seen as the life of God
which inspires creation and renews it (Psalm 104.30; Job 33.4;
John 6.33; Romans 8.2). We should not, however, overdo these
distinctions for the Word is also the life which is the light of all
humanity (John 1.4) and creation by God's mighty Word inspires
awe in the psalmist. It is, perhaps, worth remembering that the
Fathers thought of the harmony of Word and Spirit in creation.

The Fellowship of the Holy Spirit

Bishop John Taylor has pointed out, moreover, that the most basic
way of thinking about the Holy Spirit is not in terms of life or
power but of communion or fellowship. It is that word *koinonia*
again (2 Corinthians 13.14). The communion or fellowship is the
result of the 'in-between-ness' of the Holy Spirit. It is the Holy
Spirit who is the agent and medium of communication between
God and human beings and between human beings themselves.

Just as, in the story of creation, the Spirit is thought of as the
wind or the storm of God, so also, in the story of revelation, the
Spirit may be seen as a powerful, almost invasive, force taking hold
of people and declaring God's Word to them and through them.[4]
The Spirit inspires the prophets, for example, to speak the Word
of God to those around them at crucial moments in history.
Sometimes the prophets, such as Jeremiah, thought they were too
unworthy of the task to which they had been called (Jeremiah 1.1–
10). Inspiration overcame their resistance and impelled them to
fulfil their mission.[5] In the New Testament also the disciples,
bewildered by the Resurrection appearances and perhaps depressed
by Jesus' departure, are seized by a powerful experience of the
Holy Spirit which transforms them and drives them out to preach
the Gospel to people of various nations gathered in Jerusalem (Acts
2.1–11).

Such an experience of inspiration is not without parallels in traditional as well as 'World' religions. Indeed, as Nietzsche's experience, retold in *Thus Spake Zarathustra*, illustrates, it can happen completely outside the frame of organized religion! Nor is it a merely historical phenomenon, which happened at one time but does not happen now. Ecstatic behaviour continues to be an important part of 'folk' or 'popular' religion in many different traditions. In the history of Christianity there have been movements, from time to time, which have emphasized the importance of this kind of experience. The twentieth century itself is known for the rise of old-style pentecostal and holiness movements and, within the mainline churches, the emergence of the charismatic or renewal movements has affected Christians from many different backgrounds.

We must not imagine, however, that the work of the Spirit is *always* to be thought of in this way. Among the rabbis, for instance, the work of the Spirit is thought of primarily as inspiring the Torah which provided a God-given way to live. It is also thought of as inspiring not so much the ecstatic prophets of ancient days but the 'writing' prophets and their high moral consciousness. These views find their echoes in the New Testament as well. The New Testament writers certainly see the Hebrew Scriptures as inspired by the Spirit (Mark 12.36; Acts 1.16; 28.25; 2 Timothy 3.16; Hebrews 3.7; 2 Peter 1.21; etc.). Towards the end of the New Testament period, the New Testament writings themselves are beginning to be understood in a similar fashion (2 Peter 3.15–16; Colossians 4.16; Revelation 1.3).

The emphasis has altered then to the inspired nature of the Scriptures which provide an interpretive key for the events and experiences which had brought the early Church into existence. In Luke and John, experience of the Spirit leads to mission in the world, while in Paul, the emphasis is on the continuing 'life in the Spirit' or the 'fruit of the Spirit'. Certainly, the Spirit brings an immediacy of personal relationship with God and the possibility of free obedience and worship. This is seen, however, most clearly in the business of daily living according to the pattern of Christ.

By transforming our lives, so that they are in accord with the mind of Christ, and making it possible for us to worship God in freedom and in truth, the Spirit emerges not only as the one who communicates God's will and word to us but also as the one who makes communion with God possible. But this communion with

God is also the means by which we come into fellowship with others who have also responded to the work of the Spirit: 'For by one Spirit we were all baptized into one body – Jews or Greeks, slaves or free – and all were made to drink of one Spirit' (1 Corinthians 12.13). It is our common baptism which is the basis of this fellowship, not agreement in doctrine or some spiritual experience or the possession of a particular gift. F. F. Bruce notes the emphatic 'we all'. It is not a spiritual elite but all the members of Christ's body who are included in this blessing.[6] Increasing recognition of one another's baptism, as a result of the modern ecumenical movement, is an encouraging sign that churches are beginning to recognize the basis of their *koinonia*. The full implications of this recognition, for further agreement in faith and for sharing in each other's sacramental life, are only now being realized.

John V. Taylor has pointed out that the Holy Spirit does not *only* communicate God's Word to us nor does the Spirit *only* make fellowship possible between Christians, but the Spirit is that current of communication which makes *any* meeting possible. It has to be said, first of all, that the Eternal Spirit has been working in every age and culture to make people aware of the divine and to evoke their response. Such a response may sometimes be seen in a religious tradition or it may be seen in personal piety or even in a rejection of religion when it is seen as oppressive or exploitative. Because of human ignorance, sinfulness and rebellion this response will always be distorted and faltering, *but it will be there*. When Christians encounter people of another spiritual tradition, the Spirit working in them will evoke a response from the other in whom the Spirit is also working. Such a response will not always be in the cultural terms which Christians might expect. Christian faith is usually expressed in culturally specific ways. Today it can be expressed in a number of very different ways but Christians know also that none of these ways exhaust the meaning of Christ for the world. The acknowledgement of his Lordship may come to fruition in yet another culture, even a religious culture, in quite a different way. It is true that inter-faith dialogue is also often inter-cultural but the sensitive Christian will be able to recognize what in their culture is of the Spirit and, even more importantly, what in their inter-locutors' culture is a movement in response to the Spirit.[7]

The Economy of the Holy Spirit

It is true that the Spirit was uniquely present in all that Jesus did and taught but just as the Creator-Spirit is present and active throughout the universe, so also the Spirit as judge and saviour is universal and working in people of every kind. In his farewell discourses, Jesus promised his disciples that the Paraclete would come not only to encourage and comfort them but also to 'convince' the world of sin, righteousness and judgement (John 16.8). Much turns on what the verb *elenchein* is supposed to mean. Some translate the verb to mean that the Holy Spirit will 'convict' the world of its sin and thus see this as a judging function. Others understand it to mean that the Spirit is engaging with the consciences of men and women, bringing them to an awareness of their shortcomings and also of the possibility of repentance so that they may escape judgement. This can be seen much more as a teaching or preparing function.

While the Western Christian tradition has emphasized the work of the Logos in illumining the minds and hearts of human beings, the East has tended to understand God's universal work in bringing people to an awareness of their own sin and also of the divine reality, more in terms of what is called the *oikonomia* or the economy of the Holy Spirit. According to Metropolitan Georges Khodr of Mount Lebanon, 'the Spirit is present everywhere and fills everything by virtue of an economy distinct from that of the Son'.[8] In Orthodox thought the Word and the Spirit are regarded as the 'two hands of the Father'. The work of the Spirit is not subordinated to that of the Son and Pentecost is seen not as a continuation of the Incarnation but its sequel, having a character of its own. Pentecost is a sign that the whole of creation is permeated by the Spirit. The Orthodox recognize, nevertheless, that the economies of the Word and the Spirit are related to one another: the Word also enlightens all and the Spirit, after all, witnesses to Christ and seeks to fashion Christ within us. As Moltmann has pointed out, although the Spirit proceeds from the Father alone, as the source of the Godhead, the Father is, nevertheless, *the Father of the Son*.[9] In terms of being, the Spirit is from the Father, but in terms of relationship and of mission the Spirit is from both the Father and the Son. The Spirit 'proceeds' from the Father but 'receives' from the Son. That is why the term 'Spirit of the Son' is correct and why Jesus could say that the Spirit would be sent by both the Father and the Son (John 14.26, 16.7; cf. Romans 8.9).

The witness of the Spirit to Christ may certainly be seen through the Spirit's work in the Church, particularly as the Church itself bears witness to all that God has done in Christ. It may, however, be seen beyond the boundaries of the Church. The well-known evangelical Anglican, Sir Norman Anderson, believed that the Holy Spirit could influence men and women outside the Christian faith in such a way that they came to recognize their own sinfulness and need for forgiveness. He believed, moreover, that such people could find forgiveness and peace in this life and, on the other side of the grave, would be able to recognize the source of the mercy they had experienced on earth. His deep knowledge of the Islamic world had made him aware that there were people of deep spirituality in that world who were sincere seekers after God and worshippers of him.[10] Kenneth Cracknell remarks that such an attitude takes Sir Norman very close indeed to the Orthodox position described earlier.[11]

A recognition of the universal work of the Spirit leads the Orthodox to acknowledge that not only individual men and women but faith systems as such can be regarded as points where the energies and the inspiration of the Holy Spirit are at work.[12] John Taylor, on the other hand, sees the Spirit not so much as operating *within* the religions as eliciting a response from them. For him, a religion is a tradition of response to an awareness created by the Holy Spirit.[13] Neither of these positions involve endorsing every religious tradition or every aspect of a religious tradition. Khodr admits, for example, that to discern the work of the Spirit in a particular tradition one has to penetrate beyond the symbols, historical forms and legalism to the spiritual life being nurtured there.[14] Taylor also is clear that while the historical religions retain some authentic tradition of response to the Spirit, this can be, in fact, mixed with false opinions and errors which have been brought about by the social and personal contexts in which people are brought up.[15] It should not be forgotten that historical Christianity shares these characteristics with other religions. It is true that the Christian 'traditions of response' have grown out of God's unique self-disclosure in Christ and bear witness to it. It is true also that the Church is a divine instrument through which God is fulfilling his purposes. Nevertheless, the Gospel should not be simply identified with the churches. The Gospel may be preached and lived in the churches, we pray that it is, but it cannot be confused with them. The Gospel both affirms and judges aspects of the Church's life as, indeed, it does of the other religions.

We have seen how the 'convincing' or 'convicting' work of the Holy Spirit brings people to an awareness of their condition, to repentance and to new life. This may come about through the 'ordinary' means of grace as found in the Church's preaching and its sacramental life, or it may come through 'extraordinary' means in the context of another religious tradition or in some other way. It is, perhaps, worth saying at this point that 'extraordinary' does not mean unusual or rare but simply that 'conversion' of this kind takes place outside the structures of Salvation History as they are known through our reading of the Bible and in the history of the Christian Church. It is also true, of course, that this 'normative' Salvation History itself bears witness to numerous other 'salvation histories' which can be discerned in its light.[16]

For many years now, Bishop John Taylor, in conversation, correspondence and publication, has been arguing for the possibility of the 'conversion' of religious traditions. It is true, of course, that the historical religions influence one another. They do not exist in sanitized compartments where they can be studied in isolation from each other. They exist, rather, in the hurly-burly of life where they often come into contact with one another and influence one another for good or for ill. Taylor is aware, for instance, of the significant impact which Christianity has had on Hinduism and the ways in which this has changed the latter.[17] Sufism or Islamic mysticism, similarly, emerged and developed in profound interaction with the desert spirituality of the hermits and monks of Syria and Egypt.[18] At the same time, we can say that Islam has made a lasting impression on Christianity through its mediation of ancient learning to the universities of Western Europe, that Hinduism and Buddhism remind Christians of the need to respect the non-human creation and that Judaism takes us back to our roots, bringing to our attention the necessity of a morally-based society.

Surely, though, the conversion of religions is more than this? The response which each tradition makes to the Spirit should be purified in such a way that false accretions fall away, corruptions are set aside and areas of neglect addressed. At the same time, each response will be made in terms of all that is God-given and Spirit-filled in a particular tradition. In this way we can, perhaps, begin to speak of the Spirit leading all 'traditions of response' to conversion to God.

It is important, at this point, to state that the authenticity of such a 'conversion' and its extent can be discerned by Christians only in terms of its approximation to the paradigm of God's self-revelation in Christ and its orientation towards fulfilment in Christ.[19] Indeed we can say that it is possible to discern the Spirit's work in others only insofar as it is possible to discern Christ-likeness among them. This may be the Christ-likeness of love and forbearance, of suffering and forgiveness or of generosity and peace. It is true that God is working out his purposes in many different ways but through reflection, crisis and conversion each tradition of response will be brought to fulfilment in Christ, as, indeed, will the rest of creation (Ephesians 1.10).

The Creating and Comforting Spirit

The very word in Genesis 1.2 which is translated 'stirring' for the agitating work of the Holy Spirit, can also, of course, be translated as 'brooding', giving the sense not only of creating but of *nurturing*. In the deutero-canonical books of the Apocrypha, the Spirit is spoken of as 'filling the whole earth', holding everything together and making creativity possible (Wisdom 1.7 ff.). It is this sense of the Spirit's creative and sustaining work which has led poets such as Gerard Manley Hopkins to reflect on the relation of the Spirit to the constant renewal of creation:

> And for all this, nature is never spent;
> there lives the dearest freshness deep down things;
> And though the last lights of the black West went
> Oh, morning, at the brown brink eastward, springs —
> Because the Holy Ghost over the bent
> World broods with warm breast and with Ah! bright wings.[20]

As John Taylor has finely said, 'The Spirit of Life is ever at work in nature, in history and in human living, and wherever there is a flagging or corruption or self-destruction in God's handiwork, he is present to renew and energize and create again.'[21]

We have seen already how the Spirit is, at the same time, God's movement which attracts men and women to himself as well as that which makes their response possible. Augustine and the Reformers emphasized the importance of the Spirit's prior work in calling sinners to repentance and in the renewal of their lives which is the basis of 'all true conversion. Here also the Spirit does not only create or recreate but nurtures, comforts and cares for the believer. The Comforter is an important title for the Spirit (John 14.16 *et al.*) It certainly means that the Spirit brings assurance of salvation to those who have responded to God's love and it also means that the Spirit sustains us in our life of faith, no matter what difficulties and disappointments we have to face. But, of course, *Parakletos*, or Paraclete, means much more than that. It is sometimes translated 'advocate' or 'counsellor'.

Commentators tell us that this need not mean a 'lawyer' or an 'attorney' in the technical sense but it does have the sense of a helper or mediator pleading for us. St Paul tells us, for example, that the Spirit intercedes for us and makes it possible for us to make the Christian confession, calling God 'Abba' or Father (Romans 8.16–17, 26–7). It is, perhaps, interesting that the only other explicit reference to 'the Paraclete', outside St John's Gospel, is in 1 John 2.1 and that is a reference to Jesus Christ and *his* intercessory work (cf. Hebrews 7.25, 9.24; *et al.*) The Spirit then is 'another' Comforter to plead on our behalf, to unite us with the Father and the Son and to encourage us in the Christian life. It is true that normative Christian prayer is to the Father, through the Son and in the Spirit. There are, however, examples of prayers *to* the Son in the New Testament and early Christian writings, especially, of course, the *marana-tha*, 'Our Lord, Come!' which occurs not only in Paul (1 Corinthians 16.22) and in Revelation 22.20 but also as part of an early eucharistic liturgy in the *Didache*. The Aramaic form was retained because it was both primitive and well-known. F. F. Bruce comments, 'It is a testimony to the place given to the exalted and expected Christ in the worship of the most primitive church.'[22] In the same way, while direct invocation of the Holy Spirit is rare in the Christian tradition, it is worth noting that *paraclete* originally meant 'one who is called to someone's aid'. It may well be in order, therefore, to invoke the assistance of the Paraclete in times of especial need and, particularly, when we are preparing ourselves for 'access to the Father' (Ephesians 2.18).

Is the Holy Spirit a Person?

Should the Holy Spirit be understood as an energy or impersonal force or as a divine person, like the Father and the Son? The Scriptural evidence *appears* to be ambiguous. The terms *ruach* in Hebrew and Aramaic and the Greek *pneuma* can suggest an impersonal, wind-like force blowing at God's command. Many scholars believe that the Spirit's personality cannot be directly read out of the Old Testament, while others are of the view that in Paul 'every approach to a personalisation of the Spirit is lacking'.[23] Yet from the time of St Basil of Caesarea there have been champions of the Spirit's personhood. According to him, this may be seen in the Spirit's glorification of the Son (John 16.14) which is also the glorification of the Father (Philippians 2.10–11). It is seen also in the dominical teaching about blaspheming against the Spirit (Mark 3.28–9). Blasphemy, for him, can only be against persons and whatever pertains to them. The Spirit personally directs the mission of the infant Church (Acts 10.20, 13.2, 16.7, 21.11, *et al.*), brings to remembrance the teaching of Jesus and guides the disciples into all truth (John 14.26, 16.13). The Spirit's guidance can be resisted and the Spirit can be grieved and even angered (Isaiah 63.10; Micah 2.7; cf Eph. 4.30). But the Spirit also intercedes for God's people with sighs and groans too deep for words (Romans 8.26). For Basil, the Holy Spirit is not 'a ministering angel' or a created force because the Scripture itself refers to 'the Lord who is the Spirit' (2 Corinthians 3.17–18). The Holy Spirit is the third Person of the Blessed Trinity and co-exists eternally with the Father and the Son. The Spirit not only glorifies the Father and the Son but is glorified in the church's doxology. In his church, Basil used two forms of the doxology: one which ascribed 'Glory to the Father through (*dia*) the Son in (*en*) the Holy Spirit' and the other which spoke of 'Glory to the Father with (*meta*) the Son and with (*sun*) the Holy Spirit'. The former was more usual in the Greek-speaking churches while the latter was traditional in many of the non-Greek, oriental churches with which Basil was familiar.[24]

It is interesting that the very scholar who questions the personality of the Spirit in Paul, is also able to say that in the Johannine writings the ground is slowly being prepared for the notion of the Holy Spirit as a person.[25] This is supported by the New Testament scholar, C. K. Barrett, who holds that the use of the masculine

Parakletos itself tends to remove the Spirit from the sphere of an abstract, impersonal force into that of personhood. He finds that a fully personal view of the Spirit is developed in the last discourses of St John's Gospel and it is here that the groundwork for the later doctrine of the Trinity is laid.[26] From Basil we know that the idea of personalized and even divine personhood is not entirely absent from St Paul's writings either.

In this connection, it is, perhaps, interesting to observe that Moltmann also bases his view of the Spirit's personality on the Spirit's glorification of Jesus as Lord and the glorification of the Father through Jesus. According to Moltmann, the Spirit glorifies the Father and the Son by fulfilling their mission of reconciliation in the world. The Father and the Son are glorified through the transformation and reconciliation of men and women who are themselves gathered up in the glorification of the Father and the Son through the Spirit. In this way the Spirit brings them into communion with the life of God himself. The Spirit then is the Person through whom the Father and the Son receive their glory, both in time and in eternity.[27]

The Holy Spirit and the Feminine

It is now a commonplace in Christian theology that God is beyond gender and that language which ascribes gender to God is doing so as a matter of convenience. Indeed, the biblical evidence is that both male and female have their origin in God and that both men and women have been created in God's image (Genesis 1.27). This must mean that both masculine and feminine metaphorical language can be used of God, though neither can be seen as exhaustive of the divine person. It is true that the cultures in which the books of the Bible came to be written were largely patriarchal and that this led to the dominance of masculine language about God. There is, nevertheless, enough to show that feminine metaphors could also be used to describe God's love and saving activity (Numbers 11.11–12; Deuteronomy 32.18; Isaiah 42.14; 46.3–4; 66.7–9).

Feminist exegetes have often pointed out that the etymologies of the words for 'womb' and 'compassion' are closely related in Semitic languages (including the biblical ones) and that the Bible sometimes speaks of God's love in terms of the womb (Isaiah 49.15; 63.15; Jeremiah 31.20; Hosea 2.23). Maternal metaphors for God arc also used in passages such as Isaiah 66.13. In the New Testament, Jesus' use of the imagery of the mother bird to portray his concern for Jerusalem is well-known (Matthew 23.37 and parallels), and reminds us of similar language in the Hebrew Bible which paints a picture of God's protection of Israel (Deuteronomy 32.11).[28] That there is further reflection on these strands in Scripture is shown, for example, in *The Prayers and Meditations of St Anselm*:

> And you Jesus, are you not also a mother?
> Are you not the mother, who like a hen,
> gathers her chickens under her wings?
> Truly, Lord, you are a mother;
> for both they who are in labour
> and they who are brought forth
> are accepted by you.[29]

In a similar way, the anchorite, Lady Julian of Norwich, speaks of God 'as really our Mother as he is our Father'. He showed this throughout, and particularly when he said that sweet word 'it is I'. In other words, 'it is I who am the strength and goodness of Fatherhood; I who am the wisdom of motherhood; I who am light and grace and blessed love; I who am Trinity; I who am Unity'.[30] According to her, everything that can appropriately be said of motherhood can be said of God. Indeed, it is in our love for God that we fully appreciate the nature of fatherhood and motherhood.

In cultures where the religious tradition has been accustomed to speaking of the divine being in both paternal and maternal terms, Christians have continued to address God in this way. So Krishna Pillai from Southern India could write:

> The God in whom the three are One
> And who is one in three
> Holy One in body, speech and mind
> In form the peerless mother of all good deeds.[31]

And from Western India, N. V. Tilak could hold both images together in a single metaphor:

> Lay me within thy lap to rest
> Around my head thine arm entwine
> Let me gaze up into thy face
> O Father-Mother mine![32]

Once it is recognized that, while paternal images of God remain dominant, maternal images also form a significant strand in Scripture, it will be possible to use terms such as 'the motherly fatherhood of God' in an attempt to do justice to both strands in Scripture and in Christian experience. Language about the Holy Spirit has to be set in the total context of language about the Godhead as a whole. Lady Julian refers to the gracious lordship of the Spirit while describing 'the motherly fatherhood of God'. According to her, this is a lordship of help and grace which gives us strength for discipleship. It is often said that the grammatical form of the term 'Holy Spirit' is feminine in Semitic languages. This certainly seems to be the case with Hebrew, though in Arabic it can be both and in Christian Aramaic it is treated as 'common gender'.[33] It is well-known that in the Greek *pneuma* is neuter, while *parakletos* is masculine. In fact, even for *pneuma*, both neuter and masculine pronouns are used in Scripture. David Anderson, translating St Basil, chooses masculine pronouns to render the Greek neuter and in doing so seems to be following the majority of Bible translators.

Some commentators hold that grammatical gender has little to do with the way in which personality or character are imagined by people.[34] On the other hand, we have the testimony of C. K. Barrett to consider when he tells us that the use of *parakletos* 'in its grammatical form alone tends to remove the Spirit from the sphere of abstract, impersonal force into that of personality'.[35] On the principle then of 'what is sauce for the goose must also be sauce for the gander', we must ask if a masculine grammatical form leads us to speak of the Spirit in personal terms, should not a feminine grammatical form also lead us to think of the Spirit's personality in a particular way?

Feminist scholars, such as Elisabeth Schüssler Fiorenza, have drawn attention to the feminine form not only of *Ruach* (or Spirit) but of *Chokmah* (Wisdom) and *Shekinah* (or the Presence). At the very least, it is significant that such important characteristics of God in the Hebrew Bible should all be feminine; there are others, such as Word (*Dabar*) which are not. The issue cannot, however, be decided on grammatical form alone for Hebrew is a language in which qualities are often feminine as, for example, 'might' (*Geburah*) or even 'love' (*Ahabah*). We need, further, to ask if these divine characteristics are portrayed as feminine and here we will have to be on guard against the dangers of stereotyping gender-roles. Feminist theologians repeatedly warn against sentimentalizing the feminine and, perhaps more importantly, importing sexual difference within the Godhead.[36] Such warnings have to be taken with the seriousness they deserve. If, however, we can speak of God as Father and Mother (as Soskice allows), if the Son can also be spoken of as our Mother as well as our Brother (as in Julian) and if the Lord is the Spirit, then why can the Spirit not be spoken of as Mother?

Elisabeth and Jürgen Moltmann have drawn our attention to the tendency, in early Syriac Christianity, of speaking of the Holy Spirit in maternal terms. They refer to St Makarios who is supposed to have said that the Holy Spirit is our mother because we are comforted by the Spirit as a mother comforts her child (Isaiah 66.13) and because we are reborn of the Spirit (John 3.3, 5).[37] Hopkins saw the brooding, nurturing role of the Spirit not only in the original creation but also in its renewal. It can also be seen in bringing believers to new life and in their nurture in the Church. It is certainly true that 'the activity of all three can be styled in the procreative imagery of the human feminine and the human masculine' but bringing to birth, nurture and comfort are part of this imagery and, while it is not confined to the Spirit, nevertheless, the Spirit cannot be excluded from such maternal imagery. Indeed, in some linguistic and cultural contexts, such imagery may, more readily, be used of the Spirit.

Fiorenza has identified the risen Christ not only with the Spirit of God but also with the divine *Sophia* (1 Corinthians 1.24, 30; 2 Corinthians 3.17). She points out that in Semitic languages both terms are feminine, as is the term *Shekinah*. Once again, the important point is not so much the grammatical form of *Sophia* (or *Chokmah*) but how it is portrayed in the Bible and the apocryphal writings. It is clear that both in the canonical books (e.g. Proverbs 8) and in the apocryphal (e.g. Wisdom of Solomon and 1 Enoch), Wisdom is portrayed in ways that are unmistakably feminine. In the New Testament, teaching about Christ as the Eternal Word (or Logos) and as the Cosmic Saviour was developed by drawing heavily on this Wisdom tradition.[38]

The Renewing Work of the Holy Spirit

The Holy Spirit can be seen then as brooding on and nurturing both the original creation and the beginnings of new creation in the Church. Both are sustained and gently renewed. In the Church, it is seen in the deepening of devotion and worship, in reading the Bible with new eyes, in fellowship among Christians and in the impetus for unity. We cannot forget, however, that there is another side to the Spirit's work: this is the experience of 'a rushing mighty wind' which comes into the lives of individuals and communities, upsetting social and even ecclesial norms and conventions. We have seen how this almost 'invasive' aspect of the Spirit was experienced by the early Hebrews and also how the early Church was formed by it and driven out in mission. James Dunn has shown how this experience of the Spirit was fundamental to the life and worship of the early churches and how this was rooted ultimately in the experience of Jesus himself. There were, of course, differences in emphasis: Paul's understanding of the Spirit's work is, perhaps, more corporate than John's. Nearly all the New Testament writers struggle with the freedom given by the Spirit and the need to regulate the life of the Christian community.[39]

Prophecy is to be welcomed but the gift is to be exercised in an ordered way so that the Church may be built up (1 Corinthians 14.29 ff.). Glossolalia, or speaking in tongues, is characteristic of experiential religion. It can take the form of ecstatic speech which is understood by the hearers as *their* language (which may be unknown to the speaker). This is, presumably, the phenomenon recorded in Acts 2, where the people gathered together hear the apostles in their particular vernaculars. Today also, there are claims of people speaking in languages they do not know which are, nevertheless, recognized by others in the congregation.[40] Glossolalia is, more often than not, the ability to speak in non-human languages. Most commentators feel it is these which are referred to in 1 Corinthians chapters 12—14. Modern linguistic research has shown that these are not just 'gibberish' but that a linguistic pattern and rhythm are frequently discernible.

Both prophecy and glossolalia were known in the ancient religions, and 'tongues' are a feature of ecstatic behaviour in the context of many contemporary religious systems. It is for this reason that Paul insists on the importance of the source and content of the former and on the proper interpretation of the latter, if they are truly to build up the Body of Christ.[41]

Another pervasive feature of this aspect of the Spirit's activity is the 'mighty works' which are done in the name of Jesus. These include healing and meeting other kinds of human need, but also the announcement of judgement on those who persist in rebellion against God. James Dunn has shown how this kind of 'experiential Christianity' has persisted down the ages and how it has manifested itself in different movements throughout the course of history. He is aware also of the tensions between this movement and the institutional Church which has often attempted to restrict and divert this stream of Christianity.[42]

David Bebbington, on the other hand, is more interested in the way in which the charismatic movement reflects contemporary currents in culture such as the high value placed on spontaneity, the challenge to structures and the emergence of mass entertainment, especially popular music. According to him, the charismatic movement has succeeded because its time has come.[43]

The 'loss of inhibition' which characterizes much of the renewal movement has come to a crescendo in the emergence of the 'Toronto Blessing' or the 'Toronto Experience'. The usual marks of pentecostal or charismatic experience have been taken further from the raising of hands in prayer and praise, glossolalia and prophecy to falling down and remaining on the floor (being slain in the Spirit), uncontrollable laughter and even the making of animal noises such as roaring like a lion! Dr Anne Richards has pointed out that, in spite of these new phenomena, the Toronto Experience is not radically new but is of a piece with 'enthusiastic' religion down the centuries. Both she and Stanley Jebb of the Fellowship of Independent Evangelical Churches point out that there is resemblance here not only with different periods of Judaeo-Christian history but also with 'enthusiasm' in other religious traditions.[44] Richards further points out that many of the Toronto phenomena are commonplace among pentecostals in Africa, Asia and Latin America. In this assertion, she is supported by Graham Cray, though it has to be said that Hollenweger's survey of Pentecostalism in South Africa and Brazil does not reveal many enthusiastic practices beyond glossolalia, prophecy and healing.[45] Richards allows, however, that 'The Toronto Blessing' is a catch-all term and that it includes a whole range of phenomena, some of which are more obviously continuous with old-style Pentecostalism than others.

How are these phenomena to be evaluated? Indeed, to what extent can such profound personal experience be evaluated from outside? It is certainly true that the role of 'participant observers' is crucial in evaluating deeply personal experience but external assessment may also be helpful, provided it does not have an a priori, reductionist agenda. Perhaps a multi-disciplinary approach, such as Hollenweger's, which combines historical, theological, psychological and sociological studies, as well as empathy for the subject, is to be preferred.

Commentators remain concerned about *discernment* within the movement itself. Repeated injunctions not to use the mind to understand the experience and even not to pray are often cited. The paucity of the use of Scripture is another concern. Richards offers various responses to the Toronto experience. It can be seen as occasioned by a profound requirement for emotional release. If in early and two-thirds world Pentecostalism people needed to find release from the pressures of poverty, here they need to find release from the stresses of a competitive society and a work-oriented life-style. Others, especially those who have experienced the Blessing, see it as a gift from God who is preparing the Church for mission. There are yet others who are hostile to at least some aspects of the phenomena, pointing to the lack of order and discernment in the light of Scripture as the principal reasons for their objections.

Given that the phenomena are various, it is not impossible to believe that some *are* of God, given to release people from inhibitions of culture and life-style and to prepare them for mission. At the same time, there may be others which arise, in the main, from disturbances in the personality or the social context. Methodism is often cited as the precursor of many holiness and pentecostal movements. It is instructive, therefore, to note that the Wesleys did *not* endorse every aspect of enthusiasm, either in themselves or in others, but were careful and critical in their discernment.[46]

Finally, the question about the fruit of the experience has also to be tackled. Does it produce more spiritual, integrated Christians who seek to live according to God's purposes for their lives? Does the 'refreshing' and wholeness extend to all categories of people or is the phenomenon restricted to a particular class? Does it lead to a deepening of unity among Christians or is its influence divisive in the congregation and in the wider Church? Does it lead to a preaching of Christ's Cross and to an invitation to sacrificial living? As the Archbishop of Canterbury has reminded us, spiritual gifts are only made possible by Calvary. They are gifts of the Cross as much as of Pentecost.[47] Does the experience prepare the whole Church for more effective mission which is cruciform? If God has really given this gift to the Church, the proof of it must be in renewed, obedient and effective Christians. It must be in a renewed, obedient and effective Church which is able to relate to people of all kinds as it seeks to share the Good News with them.

The renewal movement as a whole needs an element of reflection within it which is not afraid to evaluate it in terms of what is best in the life and social sciences. The beginnings of this can certainly be seen in the likes of Josephine Bax, Tom Smail and Graham Cray, but more is needed. It needs also to emerge from preoccupation with internal matters to engagement with the wider world and the issues it raises for the Christian. Once again, there are examples, such as the Sojourners Community in the USA, of this happening already. Certainly holiness and pentecostal movements in Latin America give us a model for a holistic approach to the world around.[48] In addition to the socio-economic aspect of society, renewal needs also to engage in a distinctive way with the scientific, ethical, literary and artistic questions which Christians are asked. It is part of both the Church's teaching function and a vital aspect of mission, that Christians should be equipped to respond effectively to such questions. Other significant movements in the Church, such as the ecumenical and the evangelical, have through conferences, speakers and literature attempted to equip their constituencies for the world in which Christian mission is to be lived. It is time for the renewal movement to do so as well.

The Holy Spirit and People of Other Faiths

We have seen already how in rabbinic Judaism, the Holy Spirit was regarded as the Spirit of Prophecy which, with some exceptions, was seen very much as a thing of the past. The present voice of the Spirit is seen largely in the Torah and the rabbis hold that the Spirit does not speak apart from the Torah. In some communities, though, there was anticipation of the pouring out of the Spirit in the last days.

In Islam too, the Holy Spirit is mentioned in relation to the creation of the first human (Qu'rān 15.29 et al.) and also in terms of the conception of Jesus in Mary's womb (21.19 etc.) which is seen as creation de novo in much the same way as Adam's creation (3.59). Etymologically ruh in Arabic means breath just as ruach does in Hebrew and many of the Qu'rānic references speak of the Holy Spirit as God's breath. The Qu'rānic form Ruh-al-Qudus is similar to the biblical Ruach Qodesh (Q16.102; cf Psalms 51.11; Isaiah 63.10–11) and any attempts to make it mean other than 'Holy Spirit' must be resisted. It is interesting to note that both in Hebrew and Arabic, the term can have the meaning of a force which invigorates and refreshes.

In some of the Qu'rānic accounts of Jesus' birth (e.g. 19.17), the Spirit is identified with the messenger who brings news of the birth. This may have led to the popular identification of the Holy Spirit with the archangel Gabriel. It is worth noting, though, that this cannot be the sense in many other passages and that the plural form does not occur.

In four passages the Spirit is related to the Amr of God. It is said here that the Spirit proceeds from God's Amr and that this has specifically to do with equipping people for prophetic service (17.85; 16.2; 40.15; 42.52). Amr is related to the Hebrew Omer and to the Aramaic Memra which means God's Word and the latter, in particular, is a circumlocution for God's creative word which came later to be personified. This personified sense of God's Word, present already in the Hebrew Bible, stands behind the develop-ment of a Logos-Christology in Christianity, quite as much as Hellenistic ideas.

According to the Qu'rān then, the Spirit is from God's creative Word and is sent to equip God's servants and to strengthen them. Does this language remind Christians of the Last Discourses in St John's Gospel and, indeed, of the passage on the Holy Spirit in the Nicene Creed as it is used in our liturgies?

We have seen how ancient cultures with an emphasis on oral tradition in spirituality often refer to the Supreme Being as the Great or the Ever-Present Spirit. John Mbiti remarks in this context that God is referred to as Spirit because of his ubiquity and because like air or wind he cannot be seen, but his presence is felt everywhere.[49] Christian missionaries, like Bernard Mizeki, have identified this Great Spirit of African peoples, such as the *Mashona*, with the God who is Spirit of the Bible (John 4.24). It is interesting to observe that *Mwari* is now the ordinary Christian word for God in Chishona and is used in this way both in personal devotion and in public liturgy.[50] If, as we shall see, the Spirit of God is active in the world and in the hearts of men and women, it should not surprise us that there is testimony to this reality in a variety of cultures, languages and religious traditions (Acts 17.24–9).

PART TWO

*What Christians Believe
about the World*

8
What Is Man (or Woman)?

*

In the previous chapters we have considered what Christians believe about God: Father, Son and Holy Spirit. This has necessarily involved us in considering what we believe about humanity and the rest of creation. This is as it should be, for theology, anthropology and cosmology hang together and help us to make sense of the universe and of our place in it. As far as human beings are concerned, we need to recognize, of course, our continuity with the physical world and with the animal kingdom from which we have emerged. But we need also to affirm all that is distinctive about humanity. The Eastern Fathers, such as Irenaeus and Clement of Alexandria, referring back to the Genesis account that humankind was created in the image (*eikon*) of God, see this particularly in terms of spiritual awareness and moral responsibility.[1] In our day, however, we could also add the human capacity to observe, reflect upon and make sense of the universe. In other words, all that makes science possible.[2]

It is true that this image of God in humanity has to do with the potential of each individual and of the species as a whole. This is only the beginning of a process of growth and development which leads to humans becoming more and more 'like' their Creator. This likeness or *homoiosis* is understood by the Eastern Fathers as both the destiny of humans and that towards which they are made to strive. This process of maturing is assisted by the light of God's Eternal Word who gives human language, thought and art its ultimate meaning and purpose. It is assisted also by the cosmic and inward work of the Holy Spirit who enables us to respond to the spiritual reality at the heart of the universe. This is, as William Golding and others would see it, the 'glory' side of the human story: human beings have been made in the image of God and it is possible for them to reflect more and more the nature of their maker. As mystics have seen the world over, this is reflected glory but it is also really glory.

Freedom and moral responsibility imply the exercise of moral choice and, with it, the possibility of the wrong choice being made. It is, of course, the witness not only of the Judaeo-Christian tradition but of universal human experience that human beings have taken the wrong turning and made the wrong moral choice. As far as such a choice is the exercise of a God-given faculty and moves humans from the mere 'innocence' of the rest of creation, it can, indeed, be seen as a 'fall upwards' and as the *felix culpa* celebrated in the Roman Catholic liturgy for Holy Saturday:

> O truly needful sin of Adam, blotted out by the death of Christ,
> O happy fault, that merited to possess so great a Redeemer![3]

The difficulty with this 'Irenaean' position is that in its optimism it fails to take seriously the disruption and destruction caused by human sin. This is no mere misdemeanour by children which is soon forgotten in the ever-upward march of virtue. Surely, the Augustinian view which sees in sin not only deprivation of the positive good intended by God but also the depravity which is its result and also its ground, is nearer our experience of the world? John Henry Newman's analysis of our fallen world still convinces and is worth quoting in full:

> To consider the world in its length and breadth, its various history, the many races of man, their starts, their fortunes, their natural alienation, their conflicts; and their ways, habits, governments, forms of worship; their enterprises, their aimless courses, their random achievements and acquirements, the important conclusion of long-standing facts, the tokens, so faint and broken, of a superintending design, the blind evolution of what turn out to be great powers or truths, the progress of things, as if from unreasoning elements, not towards final causes, the greatness and littleness of man, his far-reaching aims, his short duration, the curtain hung over his futurity, the disappointments of life, the defeat of good, the success of evil, physical pain, mental anguish, the prevalence and intensity of sin, the pervading idolatries, the corruptions, the dreary hopeless irreligion, that condition of the whole race, so fearfully yet exactly described in the Apostle's words, 'having no hope and without God in the world', all this is a vision to dizzy and appal.[4]

It is possible to see in the passage (both the 'glory' and the 'darkness' of humanity and it is also obvious that the darkness covers or, at least, obscures the glory. Nor is the passage merely about personal sin, important as that is; Newman is well aware of the social dimension of sin, of whole societies and communities being caught up in it and of individuals, in turn, being nurtured in such fallen societies. While individuals retain responsibility for their actions, the Bible recognizes that individuals do not sin, or have the tendency to sin, *de novo*. They are, rather, born into a situation which is morally distorted and they inherit this distortion just as they inherit the language and the culture into which they are born. It may also be true that they inherit certain 'dispositions to sin', as the rabbis taught, from their parents. These may lead them to sin if the opportunity arises and if moral formation has been weak. Such 'dispositions' may have to do with the 'nurture' of children, but it is just possible that they may be genetic in origin and, therefore, hereditary in that sense. It is also true, of course, that offspring may inherit, in mind and body, the consequences of their parents' wrong doing, for example, as a result of drugs-related or sexual abuse. 'Original sin' then becomes the total context to which individuals belong and from which they inherit in a number of ways. There is in both an endemic bias or tendency to sin which leads them to *actual* sin and to the guilt which accrues from it. The image of God is tarnished and they are distracted from following in the way which leads them to being more and more in the likeness of God.

Such an endemic view of sin, in the individual and in society, lies at the root of the Christian emphasis on *metanoia*. If there is to be any conversion of the individual and transformation of society, we need, first of all, to wake up to our true condition and then, with God's help, to restore God's image in ourselves and in our societies so that we can grow, once more, in accordance with God's purposes and in the direction which he intends for us. It is, perhaps, worth remarking that in our spiritual journey both *anamnesis* and *metanoia* are important. The tokens, however faint and broken, of God's gracious purposes, of divine illumination, of spiritual awareness, are still there. In a fragmented and disorganized way we can recognize them and even live by them. It is *metanoia*, however, which enables us to put the jigsaw together and to see the pattern whole again.

On the one hand, then, we can see the Logos-illumined and Spirit-inspired human person, and also the deep structures of human society, manifested in language, culture and religion. On the other, we can see the corrosive and obscuring effects of personal and social sin. When we deal with human institutions, whether it is the State, institutional religion, the markets or the world of learning, we shall have to learn to be 'two-eyed'; recognizing and respecting all that is God-given and true but also being prepared to challenge and to change whatever is sinful and false.

Religion, perhaps in particular, shares in this ambivalence and, as we evaluate the role of religion in the development of culture, the apparatus of state and in peace and war, we would do well to be aware of it. It is all too easy either to see religions as the fountainhead of all moral sense and virtue or to dismiss them entirely as ancient superstitions which divide humanity unnecessarily and are at the root of many of the world's most endemic conflicts. In the chapters which follow, my aim is, rather, to achieve a more balanced stance; recognizing how religions embody much of humanity's spiritual and moral experience but seeing also their contribution to inequality, oppression and war. On the one hand, a spiritual view of the world and of human destiny is required, if societies are to have a coherent spiritual and moral vision. On the other, some of religion's pretensions, whether intellectual, social or political, need to be challenged in the name of the deeper truths for which it stands.

> It may be that the gulfs will wash us down:
> It may be we shall touch the Happy Isles.
>
> (A. Tennyson)[5]

9

Embassy, Hospitality and Dialogue: Christians and People of Other Faiths

*

Christian engagement with people of other faiths goes back to the very origins of Christianity. The Christian faith was born in a plural environment and had to relate not only to Judaism and to classical Graeco-Roman religion but also the various mystery cults of the Mediterranean world, as well as state religions such as Zoroastrianism in the Persian Empire.[1]

As an historical religion, Islam appeared not only in the seventh century of the Christian era but in an environment heavily influenced by Judaism and Christianity. From the very beginning, there was considerable social and religious (even theological!) interaction with Christianity.[2] In India, too, the Church has been present from the earliest centuries and Christians have had to find a place for themselves in a largely Hindu social and religious context.[3]

Chasms and Bridges in the Early Years

Not surprisingly, then, Christians have had to reflect on the place of other faiths and people of other faiths within the divine economy. We know that many early Christian writers were aware not only of the challenge posed by these religions but also of the possibility of building bridges between the followers of these religions and Christians so that Christians might share their good news in a way that made sense to their hearers. At the same time, Christianity came to be deeply influenced by the language, ethics and iconography of at least some of these other traditions.[4]

Bishop W. G. Young tells us of an early dialogue that the Syrian mystic Bardaisan (Bardesanes) is supposed to have had with a Zoroastrian towards the end of the second century. In classical theology, Bardaisan is often regarded as a heretic, particularly because of his supposed belief in 'astrological fatalism'. Here, however, we see him defending human freedom as a gift from God! In whatever country or culture we may find them, Christians can be distinguished because of their behaviour which is a result of obeying the law of Christ.[5]

Several centuries later, John of Damascus was a great defender of Christian Orthodoxy within the Islamic world. His work, *De Fide Orthodoxa*, was not only a summing-up of earlier patristic teaching; it was to become hugely influential in the development of both Western and Eastern theology. He is also supposed to have influenced the development of formal, or *Kalam*, theology in the Islamic world. John was the chief representative of the Christians of Damascus to the Caliph but was compelled, for reasons of his faith, to give up his office and to retire to a monastery near Jerusalem. His two dialogues with a Muslim interlocutor are well-known. In them, John discusses with his Muslim partner the nature of God and of his Word. The dialogue is vigorous, at times even polemical, yet it also assumes a certain common basis from which the argument can be conducted. For instance, it is implicitly acknowledged that the partners in dialogue are talking about the same God, however differently they may understand him. Such a style of argument is characteristic of Christians within the Muslim world who do not display the hostility of Byzantium or, indeed, of the West.[6]

Mediaeval Interaction

In the West, too, it is not too much of an exaggeration to say that Christian theology in the Middle Ages was largely shaped by the need to respond to the so-called Islamic philosophers who were re-interpreting both Neo-Platonism and Aristotle, on the one hand, and the Qu'rān on the other. It is to the great credit of St Thomas Aquinas that he not only provided an apologetic against such tendencies in his *Summa Contra Gentiles* but that he was also able to learn from these philosophers and to express the Christian faith in terms of this 'new learning'.[7] In spite of the Crusades, both the

Dominicans and the Franciscans were developing a peaceful approach to Islam and Judaism. The missionaries were expected to immerse themselves in the culture to which they were sent and to serve those in need. This 'witness of life' provided a basis for preaching the Gospel. Francis of Assisi certainly set the tone of this new approach in his visit to the Sultan Al-Malik Al-Kamil at Damietta in Egypt. He was followed by many Franciscan missionaries, not all of whom had his wisdom. Raymond Lull was a layman who had been inspired by Francis and who sought to put his teaching into practice. He was able to persuade the Church to establish centres for missionary education and he, himself, undertook many missionary journeys. During the last of these he was beaten and expelled and probably died of his injuries. The Dominicans, too, had scholars like Raymond Marti who were well-acquainted with contemporary Judaism and Islam and who developed a Christian apologetic in relation to both.

It has to be acknowledged, however, that often this 'peaceful' approach meant no more than a renunciation of armed combat. The polemical spirit was still there and the atmosphere was one of argument and counter-argument. Although these missionaries had often studied the languages of the people to whom they were sent, they lacked the sympathy and friendship which might have deepened their dialogue and enabled them to get beyond mere controversy. The Roman Catholic scholar, Jean-Marie Gaudeul, remarks of Raymond Lull that he never seemed to have any Muslim friends, only interlocutors and opponents![8]

Reformation and Counter-Reformation

Curiously enough, the Reformation did not result in much cross-cultural missionary activity. The reasons for this are complex but have to do with the close relationship to the state which many churches of the Reformation enjoyed and with a curiously dispensationalist theology: God was sovereign and could reach people if that was his will – he did not need our cooperation in this! The Great Commission, moreover, had been fulfilled by the early Church and people who remained non-Christian did so because of heedlessness and ingratitude, *not* ignorance.[9]

The Counter-Reformation in the Roman Catholic Church, on the other hand, was very missionary minded. The newly acquired dominance of the sea-routes, wrested from the Arabs, by Spain and Portugal, provided the spur to cross-cultural missionary work. The development by the Jesuits of the so-called Indian and Chinese 'rites' was an attempt to contextualize the Gospel, not only in terms of Indian or Chinese culture but also in terms of religious terminology and symbolism. The failure of these experiments is a witness to the obduracy of Christian bureaucracies in the face of the missionary task.[10]

The Modern Missionary Movement

It was not until the modern period of mission history, i.e. from the end of the eighteenth century onwards, that missionaries from the West began to take an interest, once again, in the language, literature and beliefs of other peoples and religions. Many of the earliest translations of the sacred books of these religions into European languages were made for missionary reasons. Increased knowledge of and familiarity with these traditions, however, often forced a re-evaluation of their relationship to Christianity. Missionaries like Temple Gairdner in Egypt and W. D. P. Hill in India spent long periods of time learning about the culture of a particular people before they felt able to witness to them as Christians. Such exposure led them, sometimes, to acknowledge truth in other faiths as well as devotion and moral awareness. A question that arose then had to do with the way in which such truth was related to Christ and to Christianity. The question remains with us today and is answered differently by different people. Many nineteenth century missionaries, however, began to see other faiths as a sort of *praeparatio evangelica* (a preparation for the Gospel) in the same way as the early fathers had seen not only Judaism but also aspects of classical philosophy, poetry and religion. If other faiths are a preparation for the Gospel, then the latter is a fulfilment of the former. Missionaries such as J. N. Farquhar summed up this attitude when they were able to discern themes and concerns in another faith which pointed to a fulfilment in Christ. Such thinking drew on the Irenaean tradition of *anakephalaiosis* or recapitulation which sees all human history with its hopes and aspirations summed up in Christ (Ephesians 1.10).[11]

The Oriental Experience

We should not forget, of course, that while Western missionaries were engaging with people of other faiths, perhaps for the first time, Christians of the Ancient Oriental, Orthodox and Eastern-rite Catholic Churches in the Middle East, Central Asia, India and Ethiopia continued to be witnesses to the Gospel among their neighbours of other faiths. There is much to learn from their history.[12]

In the same way, many indigenous Christians from churches founded by Western missions were also engaging with their compatriots of another faith. The long history of Indian Christian theologians and their approaches to Hinduism is a case in point.[13] Another example is that of theologians from a Muslim background in North India and what is now Pakistan. Even though their approach was somewhat polemical, they were able to engage with Islam at a fairly deep level.[14] The experience of these churches permeates the whole of this chapter.

Ecumenical Consciousness and Inter-faith Questions

The modern ecumenical movement began because there was a desire to bear a united witness to Christ in a world that was being recognized as increasingly plural. Since the first world missionary conference, which was also the first ecumenical conference of its kind, Edinburgh 1910, there has been a concern to relate the Christian message to people of other faiths. This concern has been expressed with increasing urgency throughout the twentieth century, not least because relations between the different religions are seen as crucial, not only to world peace, but to peace regionally and even locally.[15] Different conferences have called for a serious study of and engagement with the world's religions, while recognizing the distinctive nature of Gospel, and for dialogue to promote mutual understanding and respect.

The Second Vatican Council heralded the arrival of ecumenism in the Roman Catholic Church. The Council was aware, however, that its agenda could not be limited to the renewal of that Church and the beginning of dialogue with other Churches and ecclesial bodies. A truly universal Church must recognize the presence of other faiths in the world. It appears that, at first, there were no plans to issue a document on non-Christian religions. Pope John XXIII was keen, however, to heal the wounds of anti-Semitism and wanted the Council to develop a more positive view of Jewish–Christian relations. It was realized very quickly, however, that it would be difficult to address Judaism without also relating to Islam. This led to the rewriting of the document in such a way that all the great religions of the world were included. Michael Barnes comments that the document, *Nostra Aetate*, appears to be rather brief with bland statements about the world's religions. According to him, nothing very remarkable is said. What *is* remarkable is that anything is said at all.

Such a judgement is, perhaps, too harsh. The document attempts to set out a history of salvation which certainly recognizes God's acts among his Chosen People and, specifically, in Christ as central, but it also attempts to find a place for other religious traditions within such a scheme. God's saving design is revealed in Christ but extends to all. Other religions may display knowledge of God derived not only from creation and from conscience but also from their particular religious experience. The Church should reject nothing which is true and holy in these religions. This truth and holiness are related to Christ as the Eternal Logos who is definitively revealed in Jesus of Nazareth but who also enlightens all human beings.[16]

Regarding the Jewish people, the Council and succeeding documents are at pains to emphasize the organic relation of the Church to Judaism. The 'mystery of the Church' involves the 'mystery of Israel'. The scriptures, liturgy and history have all to be understood in the light of this relationship. The special relationship is symbolized by joining the Commission on Religious Relations with the Jews to the Secretariat for Promoting Christian Unity, and the hope is expressed that these relations will be strengthened in collaboration with other Christians.[17]

The Anglican Communion and People of Other Faiths

Within the Anglican Communion, too, Lambeth Conferences have, since 1897, considered the question of relations with people of other faiths. Sometimes their concern has been the preparation of churches for the fulfilment of their missionary obligations, at other times it has been to uphold some principle of freedom of religion or of access to holy places.[18] In more recent years, the conferences have given particular attention to the question of dialogue between people of different faiths, and in 1988 the Conference not only agreed a resolution on Inter-faith dialogue which reflected the concerns of various ecumenical statements on the subject, but also commended a document, *Jews, Christians and Muslims: the Way of Dialogue*, written during the Conference, for study and action in the Churches of the Anglican Communion.[19]

Preparations for the 1998 Conference have suggested so far that this is an issue for nearly every 'cluster' of provinces which has met to highlight important elements in the agenda for the Conference. The reasons for this phenomenon are very complex and have to do with a world of increasing mobility as well as of many conflicts, local, regional and global, in which religion plays a part.

The Need for Dialogue

In some parts of the world, Christians have lived 'cheek by jowl' with people of other faiths for centuries. The need for greater national integration and harmony has, however, made the task of dialogue even more urgent. On the one hand, Christians have realized that they need to learn from people of other faiths, if they are to express their faith, in terms of worship and witness, in ways that are authentic to the culture and the idiom in which they live. Jyoti Sahi is an Indian Christian artist who attempts to convey insights of the Gospel in ways which draw upon Indian (even Hindu) themes. In a book (with Paul Middleton), he has also provided a study of how 'sacred space' is being understood by the churches in India in relation to the cultural and religious values of the people of India. In particular, these have to do with holy places being, what Michael Ipgrave has called, 'places of mystery, memory and meeting'. It is interesting, in this connection, to note that the desire to 'contextualize' in this way is not just a concern of those churches in India which have their origins in the Western tradition, but also of those which spring from an ancient oriental background.[20]

It is not only Christians, however, who have felt the need to learn from others. Dr M. M. Thomas, the doyen of Indian theologians, has drawn our attention to the acknowledged Christ of the Indian Renaissance. According to him, although this recognition is partial and inadequate, it is important, for the sake of the Church's mission, that it should be understood and evaluated. In his work, he has tried to engage with leading Hindu reformers, such as Raja Ram Mohan Roy, Rabindranath Tagore and Mahatma Gandhi, especially in relation to their understanding of the meaning of Jesus Christ and of Christianity for religion and society in contemporary India. Dr Thomas also discusses the response of leading Indian theologians to the ideas of these Hindu leaders and points out that the course of Indian Christian theology has been definitely affected by this acknowledgement of Christ within Hinduism itself.[21]

The Situation in the West

People of other faiths, especially Jews and Muslims, have lived in western countries for a long time. This presence has, in recent years, been significantly augmented by immigration, whether for economic or political reasons. The second- and, in some cases, third-generation descendants of immigrants have, moreover, been born in the West and share its values and outlook in a number of ways. Christians in western countries have faced, therefore, a two-pronged situation: on the one hand, they have experienced other faiths as part of the 'strangeness' of their new neighbours. On the other, they are now experiencing it as the 'difference' of their friend at school or colleague at work with whom they have a great deal in common.

Since many people of other faiths are also ethnically different, this has sometimes caused confusion between race and faith. Parents want their children educated in 'the white man's religion', i.e. Christianity; and Asians, in particular, are assumed to belong to another faith. A bishop arriving from Pakistan for the last Lambeth Conference, for example, was asked if he was a 'Muslim' bishop!

Perhaps more importantly, people identify *culture* with faith so that people belonging to a certain culture are also assumed to belong to a particular faith. The term 'multi-cultural' often means 'multi-faith' as well. The worldwide nature of the Christian Church and the fact that there are Christians of widely differing cultures often comes as a surprise.

In spite of such difficulties and confusions, however, Christians in the West have sought to relate to people of other faiths in a number of ways. There are several possible categories in which these different approaches can be classified. Bishop Kenneth Cragg has suggested that 'embassy' and 'hospitality' are two fundamental categories for thinking about mission. Hospitality has to do with welcoming people and meeting their needs; embassy, with going out to them and sharing the Gospel with them.[22] Another way of thinking about mission has to do with witness, service and dialogue.

Christians in the West have tried to exercise a ministry of hospitality and of service, for example, by opening up their homes and sharing skills needed in western cultures with those of other faiths who have recently arrived in the country. Sometimes, they have made facilities, like church halls, available for social and educational purposes. The question of providing facilities for worship has been much more controversial and Christians have taken a range of positions on it. Some do not feel that any Christian premises should be made available for non-Christian worship, as, at the very least, it can confuse the wider community and make Christian identity less distinct. Others are willing for ancillary buildings, such as church halls, to be used for such worship; others will permit even the nave of a church to be used, but most of these would still not want the chancel and the sanctuary to be used.

The use of church buildings is a classic situation where western Christians can learn from the history of Christianity elsewhere. In the early days of the expansion of Islam into the Christian countries of the Middle East, for example, the new rulers sometimes took over a part of a church for their worship, leaving the rest to the Christian community. In many cases, however, the whole building was eventually taken over. The second of the Righteous Caliphs, Umar, when invited by the Patriarch Sophronius to pray in the Holy Sepulchre at the time of the capitulation of Jerusalem to the Muslims, refused to do so on the grounds that if he did so, his fellow Muslims would use this as a pretext for converting the church into a mosque! Continuing questions about the precise identity of Hagia Sophia indicate the difficulties inherent in people of different faiths using the same building for their worship.[23] In India there are one or two examples where the site of an ancient church is now used for inter-faith meeting and dialogue.[24] There are other instances, however, of sites sacred to one faith being built upon by another which have caused hostility and even violence.

The history, then, is full of ambiguities and possible difficulties. Another issue has to do with the integrity of the Christian faith itself. Church buildings are often consecrated or dedicated for Christian worship and the canons or other rules of the Church require that nothing should be done in them which is contrary to the Christian faith or dishonouring to Christ.

If this rules out the regular use of a church building by another faith, what about the disposal of redundant churches to other faith communities? If a building is surplus to requirements because the population has moved or because there is ecumenical sharing, or because there are just too many buildings, is it permissible, or even preferable, to sell the building to another faith community? Some denominations have clearly felt able to do this, sometimes on the grounds that this is better than seeing them turned into garages or warehouses. The Church of England, on the other hand, has been much more cautious. It has recognized, for example, the importance of 'sacred space' for a community. A building used for Christian worship has a certain character. This may be the physical shape of the building (many churches are cruciform in shape) or it may be the atmosphere conveyed by art or furniture or arrangements for music. Places of worship are also important as places of memory not only for the worshipping congregation but often for the wider community also. The attachment of so many non-churchgoing folk to their parish church can only be explained if the church building is seen as focusing the collective memory of a community. The possibility that some churches are built on pre-Christian sites of worship only strengthens the argument about memory.

Many hold also that the sale of a church building signals a retreat from often the neediest communities which are deprived of an important symbol of their community life. Nor are such feelings of deprivation felt only locally. Internationally, too, there may be repercussions. Churches in minority situations, and under pressure from another dominant religious tradition, may feel betrayed by Churches in the West when they hear or read about the sale of churches in this way. It is certainly true that some people are only too willing to use such situations for anti-Christian propaganda.

For all of these reasons, Church authorities should think very carefully before disposing of church buildings which they do not need. They should explore, first of all, continued *Christian* use of such buildings, whether ecumenically or by sale or lease to another Christian denomination. If this is not possible, some community use should be sought. It has to be acknowledged that in some cases a building may have to be demolished. Only when these other options have been explored, should the authorities consider disposal to another faith community, and then only after the widest consultations in the community.[25]

One of the ways in which some Christians have tried to welcome people of other faiths in their midst has been to attend their worship and to learn from it. Others have found that their friendship has led them naturally to pray with their friends, especially at times of great need or rejoicing. Such experiences have gradually led to the demand for inter-faith or multi-faith worship. In using these expressions, people often mean different things by them. An event like the one arranged by the Vatican at Assisi, for example, involved the different faith communities praying in their own groups but at the same time and in the same location. It is possible also to meditate together in silence. Then there are the gatherings of a serial nature. In these, each faith community offers a reading or a prayer. There may be a common concern or theme but no attempt is made to suggest a common activity. As Marcus Braybrooke has pointed out, 'those present are in effect an audience listening to a religious anthology in which the distinctiveness of each tradition is clearly recognized'.[26] Finally, there are the services with a common order which has been agreed beforehand. Of necessity, such services take place at the level of the lowest common denominator.

There are Christians who believe that it is *never* right to pray with someone of another faith as they may be praying to 'another god'. This may be true on some occasions, but, equally, at other times there may be an awareness on all sides of the one divine being who has created the world and ourselves and who is concerned for us. This divine being may be understood in different ways by the different traditions but, in spite of the differences, there is agreement that we are referring to the same God who has not left himself without witness anywhere (Acts 14.17).

Because Christian worship is Christ-centred, multi-faith worship of any kind can never become the regular, spiritual diet of Christians. It is possible, however, to pray with people of another faith at a critical moment in their lives. Indeed, sometimes they ask us to do this! In the same way, it may be possible to join people of another faith in times of national or local celebration or of crisis. National or local governments, embassies and voluntary organizations often organize such events (for example, on national days) and invite churches or individual Christians to participate. This is often an opportunity for witness and for dialogue. Should Christians agree to be present?

It is important that if Christians *do* take part in any event of this kind, they should be sure that nothing is done to dishonour Christ or be contrary to the Christian faith. It is to be expected, of course, that representatives of other traditions will make sure that their beliefs are respected in a similar way.[27]

In many western countries, people of other faiths may still feel themselves at a distance from the centres of power and influence. In spite of the fact that Muslims constitute the most numerous religious minority in this country, there is only one Muslim MP and even his election has been followed by difficulties of various kinds. This in spite of the fact that Muslims constitute the most numerous religious minority in this country. In a situation where people of other faiths may feel marginalized in national or local life, it is important for the Christian Churches to speak for them. Such a role of *advocacy* is even more necessary for a Church that is seen as a national or established Church. The Church of England, for instance, sees itself as an enabling agent for the greater participation of other Churches and, indeed, other faiths in national life. This may take place at a country-wide level by making sure that other Churches and representatives of other faiths are consulted, for example, about legislation relating to education or the social services. It also takes place in institutions like hospitals, prisons and universities where Anglican chaplains often make sure that chaplains from other Churches and now from other faith communities have access to their people in such institutions. The Church of England, and other Christian Churches, are also making attempts to ensure that other faith communities are appropriately represented at civic events, both nationally and locally.[28]

While Churches in the West have been active in the 'hospitality' aspects of mission, serving the needs of people of other faiths and encouraging dialogue with them, it has to be admitted that the 'embassy' side of mission has not been greatly to the fore. There are some understandable reasons for this. Christians have often felt that they generally belonged to a privileged and affluent section of society and they should not be seen as 'preying' on those who were weak and vulnerable. Some have felt, rather, that their faith obliged them to struggle *with* people of other faiths to make sure they had the same freedoms and facilities which Christians themselves enjoyed. Others have wanted to learn more about the other traditions before they felt able to witness to them.[29]

The situation is changing, however, and many people of other faiths are now in influential positions in commerce, local government and the professions. Christians, also, have acquired some experience of what others believe. It is important, therefore, for the Churches to make sure that, along with service and dialogue, the obligation to *witness* is not neglected. 'Hospitality' needs to be kept side by side with 'embassy'. Churches and Christians need to be equipped to witness sensitively, but boldly, of what God has done for us in Christ. Naturally, such witness should be in the spiritual idiom of the one to whom we are witnessing. This requires patient listening and dialogue. Indeed, dialogue can be an occasion for authentic witness, and both service and dialogue need to take place alongside witness. It is important, however, to ensure that service is not seen as proselytization by our partners and that dialogue is not an occasion for preaching at them. Each activity has its own integrity but in the *total* policy of a Church, local, national or regional, all three should have a place.[30]

Christians in other parts of the world are sometimes a mirror image of other faith communities in the western world. In countries where Christians are a minority, they sometimes experience systematic discrimination in terms of education and employment. They are often marginalized from mainstream social and political life and, on occasions, they are even persecuted for their beliefs. Christians are not, of course, alone in facing such difficulties; other minority groups face them as well. It is here that the principle of 'reciprocity' can be put forward. It should be made clear straight away that this does *not* mean 'tit for tat'. Christians should not be saying that because people of other faiths have certain freedoms in the western world, *therefore* Christians should have similar freedoms in countries where these other faiths are dominant. It is, perhaps, natural to feel like that but a more nuanced view is necessary. *The principle of reciprocity should be seen as the commitment of each faith to fundamental human rights in every part of the world.* Such a commitment should entail not just mental assent but active involvement in the promotion and defence of these rights. Respect for basic human freedoms and the rights of groups such as women and ethnic and religious minorities should be on the agenda of multilateral and bilateral dialogues.

Christian Faith in a Plural World

Awareness of the existence of faiths other than one's own has raised important questions about truth. Are all faiths a path to God? Do they all point to one transcendent reality, even though the language they use to describe it is determined by their particular historical, cultural and social context? Is there anything unique and of universal importance in the Christian faith? There are many, of course, in all the faiths who *do* believe that the different faiths all lead to the ultimate reality in their own way and that the path taken by a particular person or group is most suitable for them because of who they are, where they have been born and how they have been brought up. It has to be acknowledged that there are some who see in a religiously plural situation an opportunity to relativize all of them in such a way that none can make a personal, social or political impact. A multi-faith context is taken, then, as an excuse for marginalizing all spiritual and moral perspectives. It can also become an objection to believing at all: there are so many faiths, which one should I believe?

We have seen already that it is quite possible to acknowledge that God has revealed himself in the natural world (Acts 14.17), in people's consciences (Romans 2.15) and even in their religiosity, however far removed that may seem from a Judaeo-Christian point of view (Acts 17.22–31). At the same time, it is also possible to hold that we can recognize God's revelation in these other ways *precisely because* he has revealed himself definitively in the call, the liberation and the history of his chosen people and, supremely, of course, in the living, the dying and the rising again of Jesus of Nazareth. This history of God's judgement, as well as of his salvation, is the canon or the touchstone by which we are able to recognize God's revelation in other ways. As Bishop John Robinson once put it, to say that God is best *defined* by Christ is not to say that he is *confined* to Christ.[31]

What Does the Bible Say?

The Bible, as a record of God's dealings with the people of Israel, is mainly concerned, of course, with the experience of God's judgement and salvation among that people. It also has, however, a unique sense of the *universality* of Israel's God. Here is no mere tribal deity. The God of Israel is the Creator of Heaven and Earth and all that is in them. He is the Creator of all the nations upon earth and is the directing force in their destinies. The election of Israel means, therefore, that God's purposes for all are especially focused and highlighted in Israel. The world, not Israel alone, is the stage of God's action.

The Bible is a very complex and very diverse collection of documents which were originally composed for different reasons in a variety of contexts, cultures and languages. Although there is an underlying unity, there is also a great variety in the Bible's responses to many questions, including that of relations with people of other faiths.[32]

Not all religion is good and in the Bible there is a negative response to bad religion. Those working on the sociology of the Bible tell us that early Israel was a 'flat', non-hierarchical and egalitarian society. This was certainly because of their experience of God who had so dramatically freed them from slavery in Egypt, revealed his will for them in the desert and welded them into a nation during their years of wandering. When they entered Canaan, they encountered an oppressive and hierarchical society in which throne and temple collaborated. The defeat and destruction of the Canaanite city-states, at the time of the conquest, is seen as God's judgement on them. Equally, Israel is judged when she emulates their behaviour.[33]

Elijah's encounter with the prophets of Baal (1 Kings 18) is the climax of a long-running hostility in the Bible to the sexually permissive, even licentious, cult of the god Baal (of whom there were many local variants). Once again, such a negative response was needed if the moral fibre of the nation was not to be completely destroyed. After the Exile, there is the example of

Ezra and Nehemiah refusing help for the rebuilding of the temple from those they perceived to have compromised themselves, and attempting to purify the nation. In both of these responses there is a fear of syncretism; that the pure worship of God would somehow be mingled with beliefs and practices which were not consonant with the revelation received by the Jewish people.

These negative responses are there in the biblical material. They may have arisen because of an encounter with inauthentic, destructive or tyrannical religion. They could also have come about because of misunderstandings, political and military rivalry and just plain greed for land. There are, however, positive approaches to those of other faiths as well. Consider the Canaanites, for instance; on the one hand, there is the rejection of an oppressive system based on elitism. On the other, there is gradual assimilation of Canaanite and other cultures and, in particular, their religious symbolism. Any fair reading of the account of the building of Solomon's temple will show the extent of such influence (1 Kings 6—9). The very building of the temple, and the placing of the ark in it, indicated a significant shift in Israel, from being desert nomads to being a settled people like their neighbours.

A more positive relationship with the Canaanites is anticipated already in the Patriarchal narratives, in the story of Melchisedek, King of Salem, encountering Abraham, father of all the faithful. The story, as it has come to us, has been reflected on and redacted, and yet what we have clearly is a Canaanite priest-king, a symbol of all that early Israel was concerned to reject, bringing bread and wine to Abraham. We are then told that Abraham makes him an offering in recognition of this priestly service! Von Rad captures the element of surprise very well when he says, 'Melchisedek, in his veneration of "God most High, maker of heaven and earth", came close to believing in the one God of the world, whom Israel alone knew. This is surely the sense of the passage ... Such a positive, tolerant evaluation of a Canaanite cult outside Israel is unparalleled in the Old Testament.' He points out that the Melchisedek motif is related to the throne of David in Psalm 110. In the Christian tradition, this gives rise to reflection on the priesthood of Christ himself which is seen as being 'according to the order of Melchisedek' (Hebrews 6.20 ff.).[34]

There is then the strange story of Balaam, the Mesopotamian

prophet who is made to prophesy for Israel, in the presence of their enemies (Numbers 22—24). Was Balaam a saint or a sinner? In other parts of the Bible, he is shown in a very bad light and comes to a very sticky end (Numbers 31.8; Deuteronomy 23.4–5; 2 Peter 2.15; Jude 11; Revelation 2.14). Nothing can detract, however, from the fact that he was inspired by God's Spirit and prophesied in an authentic way.

In more political terms, there is Cyrus who is called the Lord's anointed (or messiah!) to bring liberation to his people (Isaiah 45.1–6). In the Pentateuchal and Historical Books there are other incidents, such as the meeting between Elisha and Naaman (2 Kings 5), which suggests a certain amount of tolerance and friendly inter-action.

It is, however, in the writing prophets that a more adequate theology of God's purposes for all people is being worked out. The prophets tell us of how God has done this in the past, how he is doing it in the present and what he is to do in the future. Amos, for instance, declares that God has a purpose for and acts within the history of the various nations, both far and near. The language of the Exodus from Egypt is, moreover, used to describe God's saving plan for these peoples (Amos 9.7). From the very beginning, God has worked in this way even if people have been unaware of it.[35]

Malachi, on the other hand, speaks of the ways in which God is recognized and worshipped, however inadequately, among the nations, in some cases, in ways that are worthier than the worship of Israel itself (Malachi 1.11). From the earliest times, attempts have been made to understand the text as referring to the future (in the early Church the verse was regarded as a prophecy of the Eucharist). Even some Bible translations try to translate the verse as future but the plain sense seems to be that the prophet is referring to events that are contemporaneous with his activity.[36] In both Isaiah Chapter 19 and in the so-called Apocalypse of Isaiah (Chapters 24—27), there is a reference to a blessed community of nations. God's blessing no longer applies solely to Israel; the other nations are also blessed. Israel is the primary recipient of this blessing and also God's instrument in extending it to others. Otto Kaiser comments, 'To the extent to which people of different nations and religions are forced to become acquainted with each other and to live together, human relationships are set up which cannot and ought not to be ignored by an understanding of faith which is honest with itself.'[37] There is a reference here to the context in which the prophecy first arose, but there is also anticipation of a future which belongs to God.

Among the prophets, there are different models of how God is fulfilling his purposes among the various peoples. There is, for example, the *centripetal* model where the nations all stream to Mount Zion to join in the Jewish cult (Isaiah 2.1–4; Micah 4.1–4). It has often been a temptation for the People of God, both Jews and Christians, to think like that: God's purpose for the nations must be that they should become exactly like us! We have, however, seen already that God is working his purposes out in a variety of ways and that no one model is adequate in describing God's work.

Against the exclusion of Ezra and Nehemiah, we have the more inclusive approach of books such as Ruth, Jonah and Job. The ancient story of Ruth tells of how a Moabitess woman became the ancestress of David and thus of the Messiah himself (Ruth 4.17–22; Matthew 1.5; Luke 3.32). The book of Job is not only located in the Arabian region but has many words of Arabic origin and Job himself is not, of course, a Jew but very probably an Arab. Jonah was not sent to the Jewish people but to Nineveh, the capital of Assyria. This echoes Jesus' reminder to the people of his home town that Elijah was sent to a widow in Zarephath, even though there were many widows in Israel and that Elisha healed only Naaman the Syrian, even though there were many lepers in Israel at the time (Luke 4.24–7).

The universalism of the New Testament arises out of the response to the Gospel by the poor, the marginalized and the foreigners. We are told that the common people (*ochlos*) heard Jesus gladly (Mark 12.37). He keeps company with the sinners and outcasts of society (Matthew 9.10–13). Foreigners respond positively to the words and works of Jesus (Matthew 8.1–13; Mark 7.24–30; Luke 17.11–19; John 12.20–1). This is confirmed in the experience of the Early Church which is alerted to its worldwide mission by the response of those either on the margins of the synagogue or outside it altogether (Acts 13.44–8).[38]

Criteria and Basis for Dialogue

Why should Christians engage in dialogue with people of other faiths? Both Scripture and our experience provide criteria that God is working in the cultures and histories of all people. In different ways people respond to this divine impulse and the Bible, as the inspired record of God's saving acts, provides us with a means of discerning how God has been working in the history, the culture and the spirituality of a particular people. Awareness of the divine need not be confined to the structures of institutional religion. Indeed, it may not be found there at all! It can be a very private affair and sometimes it may be found in counter-religious movements which set out to affirm human dignity and equality and which challenge oppressive social institutions.

The Trinity and Dialogue

Our basis for dialogue should be *Trinitarian*. We enter into dialogue because we believe that all men and women have been made in God's image (Genesis 1.26–7). It is true that this image has been distorted by human sin and rebellion and stands in need of conversion (*metanoia*) but it has not been destroyed and it is possible for people to recall (*anamnesis*) something of God's intention for them and for the world *even in this state*. We may say that this possibility of discerning the signs of God in creation and conscience is the basis for natural theology.

In addition to this possibility, however, there is also *general revelation*: God has not left human beings on their own in trying to interpret the universe. The Logos, the Eternal Word of God, who provides coherence to the universe (makes it a *universe*), and who is incarnate in Jesus of Nazareth, also enlightens the hearts and minds of all human beings (John 1.9). The early Christian apologists identified the Logos with the divine Reason which holds the universe together and which provides order and stability to human societies. Its illumination may be seen in the work of those philosophers who sought to understand the world in a rational way and who taught that it was part of human destiny to use reason as a way of participating in the divine work. Although the poets were seen as obsessed with falsehood, nevertheless there were 'sparks of divine Reason' even among them, and the apologists follow Paul in trying to demonstrate the Christian God from the poetry of their time.

The morality of the Stoics and the Platonists is also recognized as reflecting the light of the Eternal Word. Even the famed Sibylline

Oracles are seen as witnessing to the truth revealed by Christ. This is not to say that these apologists were indifferent to the distinctiveness of the Christian faith or that they endorsed everything in gentile religiosity. Far from it, they were, in fact, very critical of most popular and even philosophical religion. The apologists were, however, recognizing the light of Christ wherever they saw it and used it to make their case.

The ubiquity of the Holy Spirit also makes dialogue possible. The Holy Spirit is not only the point of connection (*Anknüpfungspunkt* – a term of Emil Brunner's) between God and the human being but is also the medium in whom and through whom human beings can communicate with one another, regarding matters of ultimate concern.[39] The Johannine teaching that the Holy Spirit is in the world convincing it of sin, righteousness and judgement has been further developed in Orthodoxy. As we have seen, this is called the economy of the Holy Spirit. The Spirit is present everywhere and fills everything, inspiring people in their response to God and to Christ. For the Orthodox this can include people of other faiths. The Spirit is leading all towards the final consummation, the recapitulation of all things in Christ.[40]

Reformed traditions, too, emphasize the prior work of the Holy Spirit in that renewal and recreation of the human personality which they understand as conversion. Such a view is based on the Pauline teaching that we can discern spiritual matters only because the Spirit is already at work in us (1 Corinthians 2.14–16; 12.3; 2 Corinthians 3.4—4.6; Ephesians 1.17–20; 3.14–19). In dialogue we must assume then that the Spirit is working to convert people to God. Signs of the Spirit's work will be discerned in their consonance with the Gospel, its teaching and values, but also by the fruit of love, joy and peace. In the same way, *all* that makes for human flourishing will be seen as a response to the Spirit's impulse and guidance. All that makes for strife, hatred, intolerance and greed is clearly not of the Spirit (Galatians 5.16–24). In spite of such criteria for discerning the presence and work of the Spirit, Christians will be surprised at the way in which the Spirit can be manifest and at the places of such manifestation: the Spirit blows in sovereignty and freedom, we may catch a glimpse of the work or hear the sound but we do not fully understand the source (John 3.8).

How Does Dialogue Happen?

Dialogue happens when people who are neighbours or colleagues begin to talk to each other about their beliefs and spiritual experience. It can happen when people join together to struggle for freedom or human rights and discover that they are doing so because of their faith. Sometimes it comes about because people of different faiths are concerned about the moral and spiritual values influencing the communities in which they live. They discover that their different faiths both unite and divide them on a number of issues. From time to time people will want just to share spiritual experiences with one another. This is yet another form of dialogue.

Representatives of various faiths will sometimes arrange more formal dialogues between the leaders of the different communities or between scholars belonging to these communities. On occasions such dialogues will be limited to a specific issue or a cluster of issues. At other times they may be called to review the whole range of relations between two or more faiths. Dialogue may be bilateral, between representatives of two faith communities, or multilateral, involving people from a number of such communities. The dialogue of specialists or scholars is very important, as crucial areas of agreement or difference can be clarified in this way. People can discover that their histories and beliefs are not as far apart as they thought and, even if they are, they begin to understand the reasons for the differences a little better. For this to happen, it is vitally important that scholars should share the results of their meetings with the people of their respective communities.[41]

Through careful listening to one another, people begin to understand the cherished beliefs of each side, even if they cannot agree with them. They begin to appreciate the spiritual wellsprings which motivate people's actions, even if they cannot endorse them. The German theologian, Hans Küng, in his project on *The Religious Situation of Our Time*, has pointed out that without peace between the religions, there will be war between nations and civilizations and even *within* nations and civilizations. Peace between religions will only come about as a result of dialogue between religions and this must be based on a thorough investigation of the foundations of the religions. Indeed, we might say that such an investigation must be *part* of the dialogue.[42]

In Christian circles, an important question that has arisen has to do with the appropriateness of witness in the context of dialogue. Some Christians have shied away from witnessing in a dialogical relationship because of the fear that the partner may regard this as an abuse of dialogue and a covert way of proselytizing. It is true that dialogue *can* be abused in this way by Christians as well as people of other faiths. At the same time, it has to be recognized that dialogue would not be authentic if people did not give an account of how their faith sustains and motivates them, how it comforts them at times of trial or sorrow and how it encourages them and gives them hope. Christians will want to listen respectfully and attentively to their partners' witness but they will also want to witness to what God has done for them in Jesus Christ. It is, perhaps, worth quoting, at length, a statement from the World Council of Churches' *Guidelines on Dialogue*:

> . . . We do not see dialogue and the giving of witness as standing in any contradiction to one another. Indeed, as Christians enter dialogue with their commitment to Jesus Christ, time and again the relationship of dialogue gives opportunity for authentic witness. Thus, to the member Churches of the WCC we feel able, with integrity, to commend the way of dialogue as one in which Jesus Christ can be confessed in the world today; at the same time, we feel able, with integrity, to assure our partners in dialogue that we come not as manipulators but as fellow pilgrims, to speak with them of what we believe God to have done in Jesus Christ who has gone before us, but whom we seek to meet anew in dialogue.[43]

Fundamentalism, Religion and Ideology

There are circumstances, of course, when dialogue is *not* possible or appropriate. Like other aspects of human life, religion can and does go wrong. Because of its importance to human culture and societies, such pathological religion can influence important areas of individual and social behaviour. Indeed, it can affect relations between communities and nations: one aspect of such behaviour, in recent times, has been the role of religion in resurgent ethnic or national chauvinism. Religions have been made part of, even basic to, ethnic or national identity from which others are excluded. This seems to be the case, for example, with those extremist Hindu organizations which want to identify being Indian with being

Hindu, thus excluding large numbers of Muslims, Christians and others from participation in national life. Many of the ethnic conflicts in Eastern Europe or the Caucasus, for example, have a religious component. In many cases, both the oppressors and the oppressed understand themselves with reference to a religious tradition.

Often chauvinistic manifestations of religion are confused with fundamentalism. It is true that there are some similarities. Both, for example, can function as ideologies for communal programmes and both share in some of the characteristics which Martyn Percy claims define fundamentalism. These include what he calls 'backward-looking legitimation' of present practices or experience by an appeal to specific elements in the tradition, counter-cultural rather than culture-affirming attitudes and tendencies, or habits of mind, which tend to impose beliefs and values rather than share them with others.[44]

Fundamentalism, in the narrower sense, is, however, quite often a movement among 'people of the book'. Elsewhere, I have described it as 'a literal understanding of the primary documents of a faith and a desire to apply their moral, cultural and legal demands in their entirety without sufficient attention to the contexts in which believers have to live'.[45] It is interesting, in this connection, to observe that Judaism, Christianity and Islam all emerge as faiths which are experiencing a surge of fundamentalism at this time. In Christianity, fundamentalist movements have often emphasized personal piety and ethical behaviour in the light of what has been seen as biblical teaching. In some cases, this has extended to social concern, but movements like 'the moral majority' in the United States of America and R. J. Rushdoony's 'reconstructionism' which have produced detailed political and legal programmes, are comparatively rare and recent.[46] In Judaism, too, fundamentalists have concentrated on instruction and observance within the community and in families and individuals. In the State of Israel, however, fundamentalist attitudes have led to detailed political and social programmes. It is in Islam, though, that movements have emerged which have developed ideologies which are not only comprehensive but even coercive.

Such ideologies have either a conservative or a revolutionary basis. In some cases, they legitimize an existing social and political order. In other cases, they struggle against an allegedly corrupt or oppressive system. These ideologies not only see Islam as influencing every area of personal and social behaviour (other faiths also claim to do this), but they seek to provide detailed legislation for such behaviour. This often results in the restriction of choice and the loss of flexibility for society as a whole, and it seriously affects the freedoms of groups such as women and religious minorities.

There are many complex reasons for the emergence of this phenomenon in the world of Islam at this time. They include a very large young population in many Muslim communities which is alienated from the mainstream in terms of education, employment and business opportunities. There is a continuing reaction to the experience of colonialism and neo-colonialism. The emergence of the state of Israel and the subsequent conflict with neighbouring peoples and countries are also factors, as are super-power politics in particular regions (e.g. in Central and South Asia). The failure of both 'command' and 'free-market' economies to deliver prosperous societies and accountable governments has contributed to the search for another, authentically Islamic, way. In countries where Muslims are a minority, they have often experienced marginalization and even discrimination. This has sometimes had the effect of radicalizing their politics in a fundamentalist direction. This has especially been the case with the young who have lost confidence in existing systems and structures. Fundamentalist movements offer them community, hope and the possibility of a struggle to bring about change. They can also isolate them and make it more difficult for them to relate to the wider society around them.

It is often the case that dialogue, of a limited kind, can take place even with representatives of such movements. Christians will, however, need to relate to them in other ways as well. It may be possible, for example, for Christians or churches to act as *mediators* in the resolution of conflicts where such movements are a party to conflict. In some cases it has been shown that people in such movements have a certain respect for others with a religious commitment of their own. Christians may also find that they are advocates either *for* members of such movements, if their fundamental rights are being violated, or *against* these movements if they are violating the fundamental rights of others. It is important, also, to encourage people of all faiths to put their texts and traditions in historical and cultural contexts, while continuing to recognize them as authoritative. Legal and judicial traditions, similarly, should be seen as capable of reform and development in the light of authoritative texts. Failure to appreciate the need for this can result in great suffering for many. If a political, social or economic system is the cause of significant oppression, Christians should be prepared to bring this to the attention of local, national and international organizations, *whatever the ideological basis of such a system.*

We have seen then that the Church has a long history of relating to people of other faiths and that there are significant resources for such work. The history has both positive and negative aspects to it and critical reflection is necessary to assist us in our task today. We have considered especially the witness of the Scriptures and of the early Church and have sought to develop criteria and a basis for dialogue from these witnesses. The practice of dialogue and its appropriateness in various situations has also been discussed and we have ended with some reflection on religion as ideology. We have sought to rehearse briefly the theological and historical factors affecting the encounter between people of different faiths, but we have tried also to reflect a little on the programmatic aspects of this encounter.

10
Religion and Conflict in the World Today

*

It is being widely recognized that, since the end of the Cold War, people are becoming much more conscious of their identity as a group with a common history and culture. Although such consciousness is clearly more defined today than it has been in the recent past, in fact the importance of group identity has always been a factor in relations between groups at any level, local, national or global.

Comprehensive, Cohesive, Corrective and Constructive

Needless to say, religion has played a significant part in the very shaping of the cultures and histories on which such identities are based. The scope of religious influence tends, moreover, to be *comprehensive*. Religion seeks to influence the *whole* of life and although different religions do this differently, the concerns are very similar. Some religions seek to influence society through the inspiration provided by an overall moral vision which is then worked out in terms of 'middle axioms' which can direct social, political and economic policy. For example, a general principle that violence should not be used to settle disputes except in self-defence, to protect the innocent, or to overthrow tyranny, has to be carefully worked out in terms of 'just war theory'. This would specify the conditions under which violence may be justified; for instance, the rightness of the cause, proper moral and legal authority for the action, whether there is a good chance of success and whether the evil caused by the war will not be greater than the evil it is designed to remove. Other religions influence society through a pervasive devotional or ritual tradition. Traditional aspects of Indic religions may provide instances of such influence. Yet others, such as orthodox Judaism and Islam, may supply complete and detailed moral, legal and ritual codes by which society is to be organized.

Religions are not only comprehensive in the scope of their influence, they also often provide the cement which holds together the different elements of a community. Sociologists sometimes term this 'the social function' of religion and it can be seen clearly in certain forms of traditional society. Religion is a *cohesive* force in such societies as it provides the world view, values and ritual which underpin all expressions of social life. It is not, however, only in traditional societies that religion is a cohesive force. Samuel P. Huntington in his book *The Clash of Civilisations* points to the formative and cohesive role of religion in each of the civilizations he has identified.[1]

While religion provides the cohesion needed for the integration and proper functioning of society, it can also provide a *prophetic or critical principle* by which a society's fidelity to its own beliefs and values can be judged. The so-called prophetic religions, Judaism, Islam and Christianity, perhaps show this aspect of the function of religion in society most clearly. The writing Prophets of the Hebrew Bible, for example, were often called to pronounce judgement on the people of Israel because they had forsaken the original vision of their vocation both in terms of loving God and in terms of loving their neighbour. The Prophets called on them to renew their vision and vocation both in their faithfulness to God and in terms of justice for the oppressed, freedom for slaves and prisoners, food for the hungry and shelter for the homeless (e.g. Isaiah 5.58; 65.17–25; Amos 8.4–6; Micah 6.6–16). The Qu'rān, similarly, reminds its readers of faithlessness in the past and calls them to repentance in the present so that a new life may be possible in the future (7.65–99). Other religions may also manifest such a principle but perhaps in a somewhat different way. Hinduism, for example, because of its diffuse and assimilative character, may provide a principle of tolerance against which chauvinistic tendencies within its body politic might be judged. The Eightfold Path of the Buddha along with Buddhism's radical criticism of the caste system as well as the egalitarianism of the *sangha* are, likewise, tools for social criticism in predominantly

Buddhist societies. Religion has, therefore, not only a binding role but a corrective one.

Religion may also have a *constructive* role in the emergence and development of a culture or civilization. We know, for instance, that both Slavonic and Armenian culture developed as a result of the arrival of Christianity and the translation of the Bible and other Christian literature into the languages of the two peoples. In both cases, the translators had first to invent an alphabet before the translations could be made![2] In a similar way, the Qu'rān has exercised a formative and pervasive influence on the development of Arabic and Arab culture. Even Christian and other non-Muslim Arabs acknowledge this fact.

Religion and Conflict:
the Positive and the Pathological

Because religion can be so fundamental to a people's identity and culture, it does sometimes assume a defining character in conflict between groups. There are, of course, numerous examples which illustrate this thesis: Northern Ireland, Bosnia, Kashmir, the Holy Land, Tibet and so on. Even in the 'indifferent' West, concepts, values and practices derived from religion pervade every aspect of European and American civilization, and the West continues to define itself as 'Christian' in a particular way over and against other civilizations, including some that may also be Christian! Some analysts believe that the erosion of Christianity in Europe, in striking contrast to the United States of America, makes European civilization more exposed to internal disintegration, to external influence or even to attack![3]

Such a defining role for religion is often most obvious at watersheds in history. Many will remember the dramatic way in which the churches functioned as rallying points during the popular demonstrations against terminally-ill Communist governments in Eastern and Middle Europe. Islam became the defining characteristic of reformist movements in the Muslim world which emerged during the struggle with Western colonialism and corrupt Muslim rulers.[4] Again, although Mahatma Gandhi's spirituality may appear to be eclectic, its basic driving force was a kind of reformist Hinduism. The role of the Ethiopian Orthodox Church in the struggle of the Ethiopian people and of the Philippine Independent

Catholic Church in the struggle against Spanish colonialism are further examples of how important religion can be in the context of struggle.

While it is true that the defining role of religion in the context of struggle can be a positive one, it can also be pathological. The fragmentation of nations and communities which we are witnessing in the wake of the Cold War's coming to an end, often shows signs of ethnic and national chauvinism which has, at the very least, a religious edge to it. In the previous chapter we saw also how movements in India which attempt to identify 'Indian-ness' with 'Hindu-ness', in spite of Hinduism's broad tolerance of other traditions, also fall into this category of chauvinism with a religious core.[5]

We have seen, however, that political fundamentalism is in a different category. Here religion has been used to provide a detailed political programme which is often based on a literalistic interpretation of the sacred texts of a religious tradition. Like chauvinism, fundamentalism too is a reaction to the experience of political, economic and cultural domination. It is, however, much more clearly expressed in ideological terms and should really be treated as a political ideology, especially in the area of civil liberties. Political fundamentalism has the effect of radicalizing communities and even nations. Its movements provide a basis for identity and belonging among those who have lost hope in the current social order. These movements offer renewed hope and the possibility of significant change. At the same time, they can also 'ghettoize' whole communities and make it more difficult for them to relate to wider society.[6] Some fundamentalist movements have increased the levels of violence in communities and have been experienced as oppressive by groups such as women and religious minorities.

The Justification and Resolution of Conflict

Even a cursory look at history shows us that religions have played an important part in conflict between groups because of their centrality in group identity. Religion often defines what is at risk if a group feels threatened from within or without. Religion is, moreover, a court of appeal for the justification of conflict. Within the Christian tradition, the just war theory is frequently used to justify wars, even quite recent ones, such as the Gulf War. Such a use of the theory is sometimes legitimate but at other times the theory is invoked illegitimately to justify territorial expansion or trading advantage. The Muslim view of *jihād*, similarly, has been developed to enable the community to struggle against injustice and oppression. Some Muslim thinkers have limited its use to the struggle against social evils. Others have extended it to include the struggle against imperial domination and authoritarian rule. It cannot be denied, however, that the idea has been used, both in the past and today, as a cover for expansionist ambition.

Just as there can be appeals to religion for the justification of conflict, there can be appeals to it for its resolution. There has always been a strong pacifist tradition within Christianity which has rejected the just war theory as providing an excuse for war. It has, rather, taken its stand on the teaching of Jesus, in the Sermon on the Mount, for example, and refused to resist evil on its own terms. Some pacifist Christians declined to participate in the armed resistance of even as manifest an evil as Nazism. Whatever the justification of pacifism as a philosophy, there is certainly a great deal in the Gospels and in the early history of Christianity about *making peace*: we are not to insult our fellow human beings; before we worship, we should be reconciled with our enemies; we should not brutalize society and ourselves by repaying violence with violence; we should leave vengeance to God, and so on (Matthew 5.21–6, 38–48; Romans 12.19–21, etc.). After all, one of the beatitudes is 'Blessed are the peacemakers, for they shall be called sons of God.' Peace-makers are not simply peaceable folk who like to leave things alone. They are, rather 'doers of peace' about whom a modern commentator says, '. . . whose attitudes, words, and actions preserve friendship and understanding where it exists and restore it where it has been destroyed by human friction and strife'.[7] Both advocates of the just war theory and those committed to non-violent struggle in every situation, can, at least, agree on the need to reduce violence to the lowest possible levels. Such common ground need not involve compromise on either side as both sides believe in minimizing the use of violence.[8]

Religion and Non-Violence

The leader of a group on the margins of Islam, which has suffered much persecution, has made a strong case for Islam being a religion of persuasion and dialogue rather than conflict and coercion. Mirza Tahir Ahmad's book is based on the cumulative testimony of the Qu'rān and the *Ahadith* (traditions about the practice of the Prophet of Islam). Many Muslims, within more orthodox circles, would agree with such an analysis.[9] The well-known commentator on the Qu'rān, Abdullah Yusuf Ali, commenting on Q 2.256, remarks that 'compulsion is incompatible with religion' because religion depends upon faith and will, and these would be meaningless 'if induced by force'.[10] Indeed, many Muslims derive the very term 'Islam' from a root meaning peace or reconciliation: reconciliation with God, of course, and then reflected in God's community.

In religions of Indian origin, i.e. Jainism, Buddhism and Hinduism, the doctrine of *Ahimsa*, non-injury or non-violence, has always been important and has been instrumental in developing a respectful view of the non-human creation among the followers of these religions. In recent times, however, it has been applied in new ways by thinkers such as Mahatma Gandhi to the context of political struggle against oppression and also as a way of resisting social evils such as casteism. Martin Luther King has provided us with a Christian model for such a struggle. King was steeped in the Augustinian Christian tradition but was also deeply influenced by the Mahatma. He tried to combine the biblical teaching on love with the methods of *satyagraha* to create a basis for non-violent but vigorous struggle against the evils of racial discrimination and economic exploitation.

We need greater awareness among religious leaders, politicians and peace-makers of the principles which promote peace in the various religions. At the same time, principles which justify violence under certain circumstances, need critical examination not just of their application but of their logic. To some extent, this happened with the just war theory during and after the Gulf War. The Muslim concept of *jihād* too has been subjected to rigorous examination from time to time. The Sufis, for example, have held that the true or the greater *jihād* has to do with control of the lower appetites of the self. It is, therefore, a spiritual struggle within the self. As we have seen, others have regarded *jihād* as primarily a struggle to establish justice within a particular society or as a war of self-defence against an oppressor. In situations of violence or of impending violence, it is often useful to have an analysis of the principles underlying the justification of the conflict and, if possible, to have public debate on the issues arising from the analysis. Such a debate can, in itself, create an impetus for peace, for a non-violent resolution of the conflict or, at the very least, it can reduce the levels of violence, especially where large numbers of non-combatants are involved.

Dr Raj Thamotheram of Saferworld notes in his report on South Africa how religion played an important part, first in the struggle against apartheid, and then in the building of the New South Africa.[11] People not only acted from the depths of their religious convictions but people of different faiths *acted together*. Enabling people of different faiths to act together in the cause of peace is one of our greatest spiritual and political challenges in today's world.

Mutual Accountability and Common Action

It is perhaps worth outlining the basis for such cooperative effort. Samuel Huntington has set out his 'abstention rule' which forbids civilizations from interfering in the conflicts of other civilizations.[12] Universal religions, such as Islam or Christianity, would find such a precept hard to accept since they regard the whole world as their constituency. Much more useful is the proposal for *mutual accountability* between religions (and civilizations based on them) set out by Bishop Kenneth Cragg.[13] This cannot be limited, of course, to personalities and beliefs, but must be extended to the spiritual and moral criteria on the basis of which civilizations operate. An acknowledgement that the different civilizations are not watertight 'worlds of discourse' but are answerable to each other and at the bar of world public opinion, underlies the work of all international organizations. Such an acknowledgement should be encouraged and promoted. In the contemporary world, retreat is not possible in novel re-definitions of the Monroe doctrine!

Huntington is right, however, in his recognition that world peace cannot come from imposing Western, and particularly American, civilization on the whole world! The way of peace lies in the recognition of diversity and in the attempt to discover *commonalities*.[14] Here, of course, inter-faith dialogue has a very important part to play. It is through dialogue that we discover and strengthen our common commitment to the well-being of the environment, to fundamental liberties, to inescapable obligations and to just and compassionate societies. We have noted already Hans Küng's insight that peace between the peoples of the world will come only as a result of dialogue, understanding and harmony among the world's religions.[15]

Neither Küng nor Huntington stop at the discovery of commonality. Both urge *joint action* for the resolution of conflict and for strengthening world peace. Religions then do not need just to be in dialogue with each other. Rather, this dialogue should produce cooperative action. We have seen how people of different faiths acted together in South Africa in the struggle for justice and in the cause of national reconstruction. In less dramatic ways, this can be paralleled in many other parts of the world. In the field of relief and development, the conflicts in Bosnia and in West Asia have sometimes provided the occasion for cooperation between Christian, Muslim and secular agencies. There is considerable scope here for further work to be done.

The Value of Mediation

Many conflicts today are caused by confrontational politics and polarizing media. The worth of mediation is often under-rated and yet it can be of immense value if trusted mediators can be found. Mediation encourages careful listening on all sides and through such listening a way out can sometimes be found. It requires humility and a willingness to learn from even the most unlikely sources. Politicians, schooled in one dogma or another, and used to robust expression of their views, can sometimes find mediation alien and threatening. Mediation has a higher value in societies which do not seek to resolve every issue through public debate and where the resolution of conflict is not merely a matter between two individuals or groups but is understood as being relevant to the well-being of the whole community. The community is seen, therefore, as having a stake in the resolution of conflict through mediation or some other means.

In conflicts where religions are an element, joint mediation by leaders of the religions involved could certainly be very effective. This would be the case in local as well as in global conflicts. It would show a sceptical world that religion can be a force for peace and that religious people can work together for the common good.

11
Jubilee: a Theme for
the Millennium

*

Many people of faith believe that men and women have an inherent
dignity and a specific destiny. Christians also believe that human
beings have this dignity because they hold that all have been made
in God's image. This should lead them to affirm and to struggle for
fundamental human freedoms which arise from the specific place
humans are seen to have in the world. Christians believe also that
human beings have a vocation to grow more and more into God's
likeness. Once again, this should lead them to support and to work
for all that leads to human wholeness.

Development, Justice and the Churches

It is to do with these reasons that the churches have been involved
significantly both in the struggle for justice and in the work for
human development. As far as the latter is concerned, it is true
that at times the churches have acted melioristically and prag-
matically, seeking to improve people's lives, without asking too
many questions about the underlying causes of poverty and disease.
At other times, they have spoken out prophetically against
structural injustice (for example, in the struggle against slavery)
and have been active in movements to bring about a radical change
in societies. In many cases, their point of departure has been
repentance for the churches' own participation in oppression and
for the compromises which they have made with an unjust social
and economic order.[1]

Towards the close of the twentieth century, the churches'
involvement in development faces a quickly changing global

situation. On the one hand, there is the globalization of markets and an increase not only in world trade but in the flow of capital from one part of the world to another. Strong economies, based on manufacture and trade, are emerging in South East Asia and Central and South America. We are waiting to see, even in Africa, the results of the reintegration of South Africa into the international community. On the other hand the flows in trade and capital are mainly between the more affluent countries, and many of the poorer countries of Africa, Asia, Latin America and Eastern Europe are still left out in the cold. It is often these countries which are most heavily in debt and are either not able even to 'service' their debt or, if they are able at least to pay interest on it, are unable to sustain a basic social infrastructure of health, education and social security for their citizens.[2]

At the same time, it is also true that the geographical focus of poverty is softening. The decline of heavy manufacturing, such as shipbuilding or the motor-car industry, in the 'North' and the relocation of other kinds of manufacturing to the 'South', has resulted in significant long-term unemployment in many parts of the 'North'. This has not been helped by the recent fashion for 'downsizing' which has put increased stress on those in employ-ment, while adding significantly to the unemployed. Increasing use of technology is, furthermore, making it more difficult for the less able to find work. It is interesting, in this connection, to note that many relief and development agencies which came into existence for work in the South (and then the East), are now diverting some of their resources to the North. Local authorities too are more and more conscious of the need for community development in their areas.[3]

In the light of these circumstances, do the churches have a unifying theological theme which will provide the vision and the grounding for their continuing involvement in addressing issues of justice and of human need into the third millennium? One such theme which has been suggested is that of the biblical teaching on 'Jubilee'.

As we approach the Millennium, the word 'Jubilee' will be heard more and more frequently. Does it have a quite specific meaning or is it a more vague word meaning different things at different times?

The Jubilee in the Bible

In the Bible, Jubilee is used strictly for the fiftieth year when land is returned to its original owners, debts are remitted, slaves are freed, and fields are allowed to lie fallow (Leviticus 25.8–17). It is a time of personal, social and environmental renewal. The word has the sense of proclamation and particularly the proclamation of liberation. This certainly seems to be the sense in which it is understood in Isaiah (61.2) and in Jesus' use of this passage in his own inaugural sermon (Luke 4.19). The Hebrew term *yobel* itself seems to have connotations of both shouting and freedom.

The Jubilee is closely related to the provisions of the sabbath and the sabbatical or seventh year. All of these have to do with pausing to reflect on God's creation and on his mighty acts of deliverance. They have to do with the recognition of rest and recreation as fundamental to human well-being and they look forward to 'the Day of the Lord', the time of ultimate judgement and deliverance. The idea of the Jubilee seems to be extremely ancient and is not limited to the nation of Israel. Other nations, too, seem to have practised it, though we do not know the extent to which it was practised in biblical times. Archaeologists and sociologists of the Bible have pointed out, though, that the earlier history of Israel seems more egalitarian than the latter.[4]

The 'Jubilee Principle' Today

A prominent feature of both Jubilee and the sabbatical year is the remission of debt and the freeing of slaves (Deuteronomy 15.1–18). The two were, of course, closely related, as indebtedness was often the primary cause of enslavement. But what do these ancient provisions have to do with our post-Cold War world in which free-market capitalism seems triumphant? It is true that there cannot be any literal enactment of Jubilary provisions? Do they still provide principles for justice and fair play in our world today? Churches and Christians have begun to think of Jubilee as we approach the Millennium. Following the lead given by John Paul II in his encyclical *Tertio Millenio Adveniente*, many Christians have begun to campaign for the reduction, if not the cancellation, of international debt which seriously threatens the future of many nations.[5] In this country, Jubilee 2000 is publicizing the perilous economic condition of the most indebted countries. Even the most recent initiatives by the Paris Club, the World Bank and the IMF seem to be too little, too slow and too late. The 'miracle' of Compound Interest means that these countries have already paid more than they borrowed and yet still owe as much as they borrowed. The 'servicing' of their debt means that education, health and other basic aspects of the social infrastructure are seriously neglected. Complementing the international situation, the Bishop of Worcester, Peter Selby, has recently drawn our attention to the question of domestic debt: credit is too freely available and many are in debt beyond their ability to repay. It seems that there is a need for tightening the rules on how money is lent and to whom, as well as relief for those who cannot pay. He notes also the relationship between domestic and international debt and the origin of much of both kinds of debt in a 'culture of credit and debt'.[6]

Michael Taylor, the former Director of Christian Aid, has pointed out, however, that Jubilee is not just about the remission or reduction of debt. It is, rather, about social justice taken as a whole. It is about reversing the flow of wealth, which is usually from the poor to the rich, so that, at least for a time, *it is from the rich to the poor*. It is both a challenge to our complacency and a vision of hope founded on God's love for us and ours for our neighbours, both near and far.[7]

Apart from the remission of debt, there are some other features of the biblical Jubilee which should be noted. In the texts we are reminded that the people of Israel had to observe Jubilee because they themselves had been oppressed in Egypt. Jubilee is, therefore, also about freeing people from exploitation, low wages and bonded labour. The lot of brick-kiln workers in South Asia, among whom I worked for several years, is shockingly like the state of the Hebrews in Egypt, even down to the making of bricks (Exodus 5). The work of Anti-Slavery International and others is raising awareness about bonded and child labour among consumers and governments. Christians will want to associate themselves with such campaigns to make sure that legislation protects the vulnerable and that goods produced through these dubious means are not bought.[8] Nor are these issues only about far-away places. Even in Kent, I am told that female part-time workers are being paid £1.00, one pound sterling, per hour! This should be unacceptable in a society such as ours.

Jubilee and Belonging

Jubilee is also about the ending of alienation from property and factors of production. In biblical times, people could not be permanently alienated from their ancestral land. Since land was also an important factor of production, this meant that everyone was recognized as having a stake in the wealth-producing aspects of communal life. One of the great evils, for the prophets, was the unprincipled accumulation of wealth and property (Isaiah 5.8; Amos 2.6), whether by the State or by private individuals. At the same time, when people could live in houses they had built and eat the produce of their land, this was seen as a great good and in accordance with God's will (Isaiah 65.17–25).

Once again, the relevance of such a view of Jubilee to our own times hardly needs to be pointed out! Not only do people need to have a sense of ownership of the houses in which they live, they also need to have an economic and social stake in the community. They must feel that they belong, that they have a say in decision-making and that they will benefit, in an equitable way, from the wealth they help to produce. Even, and perhaps particularly, in quite wealthy areas in this country, the young cannot afford to remain in their own communities because of the price of property and the lack of social housing. This means that the communities become more and more eclectic clubs for the rich, whilst the young are further alienated. Adequate social housing provision is needed even in communities which *appear* not to need it!

Jubilee and the Poor of the World

Returning to the plight of the Highly Indebted Poor Countries (HIPCs), while remission of their debt is a necessary first step, it is not a panacea. We should make sure that the conditions for debt relief are not so harsh that the poor suffer. In the past, many of the so-called Structural Adjustment Programmes (SAPs) have penalized the poor in these countries by forcing a reduction in social, educational and medical provision. The requirement to increase exports, especially of raw commodities, and to limit imports, especially publicly-funded imports, also sometimes places unfair burdens on the poor. I have often observed, at close quarters, some of the unrest caused by the imposition of these SAPs. The rich elite, on both sides, have benefited from international lending and borrowing. The poor in the developing world are now paying for it. We must encourage accountability at international and national levels so that such an irresponsible enrichment of the already rich, at the expense of the poor, does not happen again.

Christian Aid's *Change the Rules* campaign has shown us that more and more of the goods we consume are from developing countries. This is good because such exports can help the economies of these countries. We need to make sure, however, that the workers who help to produce the goods receive a fair wage. Make sure your supermarket stocks goods only from those producers who pay a fair wage to their workers. Look for the increasingly visible fair trade marks!

At the time of the boom in oil prices, it was widely expected that the prices of other basic commodities, such as coffee, would also increase substantially. This has not happened. In fact, commodity prices have see-sawed wildly over the years, making economic planning a nightmare in the producer countries. Mechanisms for stabilizing prices need to be found and such prices need to be *fair*, if producers are to get a reasonable return on investment, time and labour. Both fair prices and fair wages are an important part of the Christian moral tradition and have a direct bearing on Jubilee: if people are to be free from personal and social debt over a long period of time, their economies will have to be sustainable and they will need a living wage.

Artificially high tariffs for value-added goods from developing countries will also have to be lowered. Adding value to products, such as tinning fruit, is necessary if people are to move beyond a subsistence economy, yet the tariffs in the EU and in North America are punitive for such goods. The opening up of markets, so often required by international financial institutions, can result in poor countries having to pay for manufactured goods with basic agricultural commodities. Adding value to their products, without being penalized for it, would certainly improve their balance of payments situation.

Jubilee and Renewal

Jubilee then is not just about remission of debt, however necessary that might be. It is about the moral and economic renewal of the community through giving everyone a stake in economic and political life and making sure that there is a just distribution of resources. As we approach the Millennium, let us make sure that it will not just be a time of remembering and of celebration but that it will also be a time for justice in the land and in the world. The churches have a great biblical theme to hand; let us pray that it will be used at this time for the fulfilment of God's purposes.

12
Towards a Spiritual and Moral Framework for Society

*

We began with diversity; it is fitting that we should end with it. One of the obvious facts about our society today is its diversity, not only ethnic diversity, although that has also come to be very significant, but the different ways in which people live, the different world views that they have, the different values by which they live, and this is true of the majority of the community as well as of the minorities of various kinds. Personally I revel in diversity: I like living in communities that are diverse in different ways, with people believing different things, having different cultures, looking different, eating different foods and so on. I realize that this is to some extent a matter of temperament – there are some people who like living in multi-cultural communities and some who do not like this so much. But whatever our temperaments the fact of diversity is there. It is irreversible, there is no going back on it, and any suggestions that there might be are at least nostalgic and, of course, sometimes very dangerous. So we need to acknowledge with gratitude the diversity and also the enrichment that this diversity has brought, and brings every day. But, of course, there cannot be mere diversity, there cannot be sheer diversity. If people of different kinds are going to contribute to society, to the common good then there needs to be some sharing, there needs to be some coordination, and there needs to be a framework in which we all lead our lives.

The Basis for a Common Framework

It is possible, in theory, to have a framework that is eclectic, so you pick out the good things from different sections of the community and you construct a framework. People have attempted to do this in different parts of the world. Its weakness is that it lacks depth, direction and history. In this country, of course, the traditional framework for communal living has been what we call the 'Judaeo-Christian framework' with which Islam, in particular, has many affinities. It may still be right for a multicultural and diverse community to retain a Judaeo-Christian framework.' If this is so, we need to ask what the leading values are that should flow from such a source.

The first value is that of the *integrity of creation*: creation is seen to have value in itself, not simply as raw material for human beings to work on but as a complex and finely-balanced system which deserves our respect and arouses our wonder. Secondly, there has to be recognition of the *inherent dignity of all human beings*. This is based, of course, on the fundamental biblical insight that humans have been created in the image of God but it has strong resonances with the teaching of other faiths. For example, the Qu'rān repeatedly refers to human dignity in terms of the stewardship (*khilafa*) of creation which has been entrusted to humankind (2.30, 6.165). There is then the value of *impartiality in justice*: all must have equal and speedy access to justice and there can be no discrimination in society which is based on class, wealth, gender or ethnic origin. Finally, there is the *importance of compassion* in society, especially for those who are exposed to danger and for those who have been weakened by 'the slings and arrows of outrageous fortune'. We need to organize ourselves so that such people can receive adequate support without being patronized! Justice and compassion must go hand in hand (Micah 6.8) for without a caring society, the mere administration of justice could be dry-as-dust and unfeeling, failing to meet the real needs of people. It is good that political discussion is focusing not so much on the main statutory bodies in society, such as the legislature, the judiciary and so on, but on 'civil society', the networks of family, friendship, service and campaigning which make communities work. These informal and voluntary networks are quite as important to our understanding of society as, say, the Market or Government.

Adapting the Framework

Although these values should flow from the Judaeo-Christian basis of society, one would be quite blind not to recognize that this framework has also been oppressive in certain respects and if a framework of this kind were to be maintained for a diverse community, certain qualifications have to be entered. First of all, such a framework must be *comprehensive* in scope. Whatever framework we decide for our community life, it cannot be simply about the family, or about personal morality. It will have to be interested also in issues of social morality, in political questions, it will have to say something about how the market operates and the extent to which it can be regulated. The framework should be comprehensive in its moral concerns with no blind spots.

Secondly, it should be a framework that is *not constricting*. One of the great weaknesses of world religions, all of them, is that they can reduce the spiritual vision of their founders to legalism. Examples of this can be found in many different parts of the world where religion is reduced to law. This cannot be the case for a framework for a diverse society; there has to be generosity and there has to be breadth. Thirdly, and this applies perhaps much more to the Christian aspect of this framework, it cannot be *Constantinian*. Christians will have to turn away from always claiming and monopolizing the moral high ground. This is, of course, something very difficult for people to do, to restrain themselves, to be reserved about what they might contribute and to be prepared to listen to people of other kinds. But there can be no return to a Constantinian vision where Church and State are the same thing, although looked at perhaps from different angles.

The Church of England, in particular, welcomes its special place in society, but it must see that place as a place for service and not for rule. It must see its role in establishment, for instance, as the desire of the state and of the people of this country to hear the voice of the Church in national affairs. When journalists say to me as a bishop, 'Are you meddling in political questions?' I say to them 'This is the other side to establishment!' The reason that bishops are in the House of Lords, for example, is so that they may comment on every aspect of the nation's life, not simply the religious or spiritual. The place of the Church in society has changed from age to age. It is changing now and the Church is beginning to recognize what its changed role in society ought to be.

This leads us to the next point that such a framework must not be *coercive*, causing other people to feel excluded. If the church continues to retain a special place in society it must see its place as

that of advocacy, as that of enabling the voices of others to be heard
– voices that perhaps otherwise would not be heard. The
Archbishop of Canterbury, for instance, is already involved in
representing to a very great extent the interests of other faith
communities in this country, in the corridors of power, and this is
a role that must increase, not only for the Archbishop himself, but
for other bishops and for the Church generally. Such a framework
for society must be responsive to *change*. This does not mean that it
should be changing itself all the time. We need a clear moral
framework for society that is based on lasting values and it must be
clear to people what our society stands for in terms of human
dignity, in terms of justice, in terms of equity, in terms of
compassion. But it must be a framework that is responsive to
change in a fast changing world. It cannot be based on nostalgia, it
must genuinely be responsive to the world and its changes, and not
changing colour simply because of this or that technological or
political development. Of course, the other side to all this is that
people must accept such a framework. I sometimes follow ethical
discussions about technological change and the argument that one
often hears is 'Well, we have produced this monster. Now tell us
why it is good, or not so bad!' This implies that moral thinking
occurs *after* technological development and that is not in the end
sustainable because technological development must have morality,
including social morality, at its heart.

An Enabling Framework

So far I have looked at *diversity* and how diversity may exist within a
communal moral and spiritual framework. Such a framework
should provide all citizens with the *opportunity* for realizing their
full potential. We need to make sure in this society in which we
live, diverse as it is, that people of different kinds, of different
ethnic and social backgrounds, of different abilities will all feel that
they have a stake in society. No society will be peaceful and
prosperous if a large number of its citizens feel they have no status.
Whatever the figures for trade or unemployment, most people
must feel they have a stake in society and this, of course, brings
us to opportunity: what kinds of opportunity do we mean? The
first is educational opportunity – and by educational I also mean

opportunities for training – and here the Church has a specific responsibility.

At least a third of the country's schools are in the hands of the Church and the Church has some voice in what happens there. This is absolutely crucial for the nation's future. Many of our church schools have a particular commitment to an intake of pupils that is diverse: ethnically, in terms of ability and so on. I would like the Church's educational policy to take more account of these factors. For instance, I believe that the Church has a special responsibility to foster quality non-selective secondary education. We are, of course, involved in a whole range of secondary education, in the private as well as in the state sector, but we do have a particular responsibility to provide educational opportunity at every level and also to provide entrepreneurial opportunity.

It is good that the churches are often involved in regional enterprise agencies and other organizations where people are encouraged to establish small businesses, they are given advice on how to run them and, if the business gets into trouble, there are different ways of helping them. Once again, this is vital for the prosperity of the community. *Equity of access to services* is also very important. We need to ensure that people from many different backgrounds in our communities feel that they have equal access to services, for instance to medical services, care in the community, educational matters, employment issues and so on. The churches have played a significant, if patchy, role in providing advice and support for the long term unemployed. Such a service should be provided more consistently across the board.

At the same time, churches and church-related agencies need to continue campaigning, on behalf of unemployed people, for greater training and job opportunities.

Diversity, opportunity and then *community*. As I have said, diversity needs a moral and spiritual framework but we also need to work at *community* in our everyday lives. We need continually to be bringing people together: people need to come together to discover a common vision for their own local community. What is it that they want their community to be? And what place do they see themselves as having in it? We cannot live by different and contradictory visions in the same community. I think this is quite important. Within a common vision there is room for difference but not radical diversity. People need to come together to work out for themselves what their views are on the rights and duties of a citizen. One should not, of course, talk only about rights because rights and responsibilities exist together. Once again this appears to be easier than it is because people have many different ideas about rights in particular. There are some people who feel that there ought to be a greater emphasis on community rights, whereas Western political tradition has emphasized the primacy of individual rights. Somehow we need to arrive at a solution that holds these two together so that the legitimate rights of communities, of their culture and of their religion, are recognized. On the other hand, we need to ensure that communities do not become oppressive as far as individual freedoms are concerned, for that is a real danger.

One aspect of building community is dialogue between people of different faiths. Within a wider spiritual and moral framework, we need to know how much of a common vision we can have for our local communities and for society in general. A common moral and spiritual framework will not only be a check on tyranny and injustice (elective or otherwise), it should also provide a basis for the recognition of difference and dissent in a free society.

Social survey after social survey has shown that, in spite of the decline in religious practice, there remains a reservoir of good will for a moral and spiritual vision springing from the Bible.[2] These surveys also show that, even where this vision is questioned or denied, there is nothing to replace it! Such a situation must be seized upon by the churches as an opportunity to restate the vision in the language of our times and to commend it to society at large. It is good to know that in certain areas of our common life, the churches, along with other people of good will, are addressing this urgent question.[3]

13
A Ministry of Reconciliation

✳

In the light of the situation in our fast-changing world, where people are aware more and more of what others believe, we have tried to offer an assessment of the different ways in which people apprehend the divine. This has led us to explore the spiritual aspirations and insights of people with different beliefs and world views. We have attempted then to relate these to Christian views of God the Holy Trinity.

The Trinity has also provided us with the basis and criteria for dialogue with people of other faiths and world views, as have the variety of approaches in the Bible. We have also been able to ponder the relationship between the Scriptures as the norm of divine revelation, the testimony of conscience and the order and wonder still discernible in creation. These have led us to ask how Christians should think and act in a plural world. On the one hand, they will wish to affirm the world as God's good creation and their place in it. They will want to commend a responsible stewardship of creation which enhances its beauty and usefulness. They will see all recognition of truth and love as arising out of divine inspiration and guidance. They will be able to acknowledge that there is much in every culture which makes for human flourishing.

On the other hand, they will have to recognize that the world is not perfect and that there is much suffering and waste in it. Also, they will be realistic about our human propensity for choosing the wrong and bringing great evil both upon ourselves and also on people around. This will not, however, lead them to despair for they can not only see God's goodness in the wonder of the universe and in the miracle of their own personhood but also in the special ways in which God has shown himself throughout history and, particularly, in Jesus of Nazareth. From their own experience, they will know how, in spite of their weaknesses, God continues to work in their own lives, in the corporate life of the Christian community and in the world at large.

As self- and universe-aware beings, who can change both the course of nature and of history, humans are called to be 'fellow-workers' with God in both the creative and the redemptive aspects of the divine mission. Christians will be particularly alert to the demands and the rewards of such a vocation. Nor is this awareness of a call to partnership in the *missio dei* only for Christians as individuals. The Church, as a whole, needs to be aware of the call to draw the whole of humanity into God's work of creation and redemption.

We hear often that the Church is called to be 'catholic'. By this we sometimes mean to designate the worldwide nature of the Christian Church or the relationship between the different local churches scattered throughout the world, or the need for greater unity between the different denominations. Also, when we speak of 'the Catholic Faith' we mean the faith held by Christians everywhere and at all times. These are all proper ways of speaking about the Church's *catholicity*. There is, however, another side to it and that is the mission to which the Church is called. Since God's mission is universal, the Church too is called to mission throughout the *oikoumene*. This certainly means, as is often claimed, the whole of the inhabited world, but there is evidence in the Scriptures and the Fathers to suggest that it can mean the whole of the cosmos, including, of course, all living and spiritual beings. Sharing in God's mission would mean then not only preaching the Gospel to the whole of humanity. Nor could it be restricted to working for justice and human transformation, both social and personal. It would have to be extended to the stewardship of God's creation as a whole.

The Church's calling to be 'catholic' turns out to be a very dynamic vocation: it is not only to work for the greater unity of Christians and Churches throughout the world. Nor is it only to preach the Gospel everywhere. It is also to promote understanding, reconciliation and peace among human beings wherever and in whatever way this is possible. The Churches and Christians should be willing to join in with all people of good will to identify common beliefs and values which can lead to action for peace. We salute all those who are engaged in promoting better understanding among peoples and nations, reducing the dangers of violence and 'building the peace', sometimes in seemingly hopeless situations. The catholicity of the Church then calls us to work for reconciliation in its widest sense while never forgetting that it is God who reconciles us both to himself and with each other. We have simply the privilege of being partners in the divine enterprise. God's work of reconciliation is not limited, however, even to the whole of humanity. His plan, rather, is to unite all things in Christ, whether things in heaven or things on earth (Ephesians 1.10). There is, therefore, even a cosmic dimension to catholicity!

I have tried, briefly, to indicate how Churches and Christians can join in this divine work of reconciliation, whether this is through dialogue with people of other faiths, through seeking to reduce conflict in human societies, in the task of advocacy on behalf of the poor and oppressed or in the building of community, both local and global. In all of this we remember that in Christ, God is reconciling the world to himself and has entrusted us with the task of reconciliation (2 Corinthians 5.19).

> Let thy streams of mercy blend,
> Bringing Peace without, within,
> Let the night of nature end
> With the longer night of sin.
> Let two worlds awake and cry,
> Spring has come and winter fled,
> Dark is over, dawn is nigh
> Christ is Risen from the dead!
>   (G. A. Studdert Kennedy (Woodbine Willie))[1]

Further reading

Mirza Tahir Ahmad, *Murder in the Name of Allah*, Cambridge, Lutterworth, 1989.

K. Armstrong, *A History of God*, London, Heinemann, 1993.

St Athanasius, *De Incarnatione*, Oxford, Mowbrays, 1982.

A. Atiya, *Eastern Christianity*, London, Methuen, 1968.

G. Aulen, *Christus Victor*, London, SPCK, 1950.

K. E. Bailey, *Poet and Peasant: A Literary-Cultural Approach to the Parables in Luke*, Grand Rapids, Eerdmans, 1983.

M. Barnes, *Religions in Conversation*, London, SPCK, 1989.

St Basil the Great, *On the Holy Spirit*, New York, St Vladimir's Press, 1980.

D. W. Bebbington, *Evangelicalism in Modern Britain*, London, Unwin, 1989.

J. A. Beckford and S. Gilliat, *The Church of England and Other Faiths in Multi-Faith Areas*, Coventry, University of Warwick, 1996.

K. Bediako, *Christianity in Africa: The Renewal of a Non-Western Religion*, New York, Orbis, 1995.

R. Bell, *The Origin of Islam in its Christian Environment*, London, Macmillan, 1925.

L. Boff, *Ecclesio: Genesis: The Base Communities Reinvent the Church*, London, Collins, 1986.

D. Bosch, *Transforming Mission*, New York, Orbis, 1991.

G. Carey, *The Gate of Glory*, London, Hodder, 1992.

CCBI, *Unemployment and the Future of Work*: An Enquiry for the Churches, London, CCBI, 1997.

Council of Churches for Britain and Ireland (CCBI), *Christian Identity, Witness and Inter-Faith Dialogue*, London, CCBI, 1991.

K. Cracknell, *Towards a New Relationship*, London, Epworth, 1986.

K. Cragg, *To Meet and to Greet*, London, Epworth, 1992.

K. Cragg, *The Lively Credentials of God*, London, DLT, 1995.

P. Davies, *The Mind of God*, London, Penguin, 1992.

R. Dawkins, *The Blind Watchmaker*, London, Penguin, 1988.

G. D'Costa, *Theology and Religious Pluralism*, Oxford, Blackwell, 1986.

Teilhard de Chardin, *The Phenomenon of Man*, London, Collins, 1959.

Teilhard de Chardin, *Le Milieu Divin*, London, Collins, 1960.

Teilhard de Chardin, *The Future of Man*, London, Collins, 1964.

Doctrine Commission of the Church of England, *The Mystery of Salvation*, London, Church House Publishing, 1995.

J. D. G. Dunn, *Unity and Diversity in the New Testament*, London, SCM, 1990.

J. C. England, ed., *Living Theology in Asia*, London, SCM, 1981.

G. R. Fackre, *Ecumenical Faith in Evangelical Perspective*, Grand Rapids, Eerdmans, 1993.

J. N. Farquhar, *The Crown of Hinduism*, Oxford, OUP, 1913.

E. S. Fiorenza, *In Memory of Her: A Feminist Theological Reconstruction of Christian Origins*, London, SCM, 1983.

J. M. Gaudeul, *Encounters and Clashes*, Rome, Pontifical Institute for the Study of Arabic and Islamics, 1984.

J. Goldingay, *Theological Diversity and the Authority of the Old Testament*, Grand Rapids, Eerdmans, 1987.

C. Gore, *Lux Mundi: A Series of Studies in the Religion of the Incarnation*, London, John Murray, 1889.

Dom Bede Griffiths, *Christ in India*, Springfield, ILL, Templegate, 1967.

J. Hick, *God and the Universe of Faiths*, London, Collins, 1977.

J. Hick, *Evil and the God of Love*, Basingstoke, Macmillan, 1985.

H. Hill, *Light from the East*, Toronto, Anglican Book Centre, 1988.

R. Hooker and C. Lamb, *Love the Stranger: Ministry in Multi-Faith Areas*, London, SPCK, 1993.

S. P. Huntington, *The Clash of Civilisations and the Remaking of World Order*, New York, Simon and Schuster, 1996.

Inter-faith Consultative Group, *Multi-Faith Worship?* London, CHP, 1992.

Inter-faith Consultative Group, *Communities and Buildings*, London, CHP, 1996.

M. Iqbal, *The Reconstruction of Religious Thought in Islam*, Lahore, Ashraf, 1971.

Pope John Paul II, *Redemptoris Missio: On the Permanent Validity of the Church's Missionary Mandate*, Vatican, 1990.

Pope John Paul II, *Tertio Millenio Adveniente: As the Third Millennium Draws Near*, Trinity Communications, Manassas, VA, 1994.

Pope John Paul II, *Ut Unum Sint: On Commitment to Ecumenism*, Vatican, 1995.

Julian of Norwich, *Revelations of Divine Love*, Harmondsworth, Penguin, 1966.

K. Kitamori, *Theology of the Pain of God*, London, SCM, 1966.

H. Kraemer, *The Christian Message in a Non-Christian World*, London, EPH, 1938.

H. Kung and Others, *Christianity and the World Religions*, London, SCM, 1993.

I. Linden, *Mission and Liberation in the New World Disorder*, London, USPG, 1997.

J. S. Mbiti, *Introduction to African Religion*, Nairobi, Heinemann, 1991.

Mission Theology Advisory Group, *The Search for Faith and the Witness of the Church*, London, Church House Publishing, 1996.

T. Modood, ed., *Church, State and Religious Minorities*, London, Policy Studies Institute, 1997.

J. Moltmann, *Theology of Hope*, London, SCM, 1967.

J. Moltmann, *The Crucified God*, London, SCM, 1974.

J. Moltmann, *The Trinity and the Kingdom of God*, London, SCM, 1981.

J. Moltmann, *The Coming of God*, London, SCM, 1996.

H. Montefiore, *The Probability of God*, London, SCM, 1985.

V. S. Naipaul, *India: A Million Mutinies Now*, London, Heinemann, 1990.

M. Nazir-Ali, *Islam: A Christian Perspective*, Exeter, Paternoster, 1983.

M. Nazir-Ali, *Frontiers in Muslim-Christian Encounter*, Oxford, Regum, 1987.

M. Nazir-Ali, *From Everywhere to Everywhere*, London, Collins, 1990.

M. Nazir-Ali, *Mission and Dialogue*, London, SPCK, 1995.

S. Neil, *A History of Christian Missions*, London, Penguin, 1990.

L. Newbigin, *The Gospel in a Pluralist Society*, London, SPCK, 1989.

D. Nicholls, *Deity and Domination*, London, Routledge, 1989.

W. Pannenberg, *Jesus — God and Man*, London, SCM, 1968.

R. Pannikar, *The Unknown Christ of Hinduism*, London, DLT, 1981.

D. J. Penman, *The Parables of Jesus*, Melbourne, AIO, 1985.

M. Percy, *Words, Wonders and Power*, London, SPCK, 1996.

J. Polkinghorne, *Science and Creation*, London, SPCK, 1988.

Pontifical Council for Inter-Religious Dialogue, *Dialogue and Proclamation*, Rome, *The Bulletin*, May, 1991.

K. Rahner, *Christianity and the Non-Christian Religions: Theological Investigations 5*, London, DLT, 1966.

A. Richards, *The Toronto Experience: An Exploration of Issues*, London, CHP, 1997.

J. A. T. Robinson, *Wrestling with Romans*, London, SCM, 1979.

J. A. T. Robinson, *Truth is Two-Eyed*, London, SCM, 1979.

D. J. Sahas, *John of Damascus on Islam*, Leider, Brill, 1972.

V. Samuel and C. M. N. Sugden, eds., *Sharing Jesus in the Two-Thirds World*, Bangalore, PIM, 1983.

L. Sanneh, *Translating the Message — The Missionary Impact on Culture*, New York, Orbis, 1989.

M. S. Seale, *Muslim Theology*, London, Luzac, 1964.

P. Selby, *Grace and Mortgage*, London, DLT, 1997.

E. J. Sharpe, *Not to Destroy but to Fulfil*, Uppsala, Gleerup, 1965.

J. Sobrino, *Christology at the Crossroads*, London, SCM, 1978.

J. Stambaugh and D. Balch, *The Social World of the First Christians*, London, SPCK, 1986.

G. Steiner, *Real Presences*, London, Faber and Faber, 1989.

G. Steiner, *Errata: An Examined Life*, London, Weidenfeld and Nicolson, 1997.

R. Swinburne, *Is There a God?* Oxford, OUP, 1996.

J. V. Taylor, *The Primal Vision: Christian Presence and African Religion*, London, SCM, 1963.

J. V. Taylor, *The Go-Between God*, London, SCM, 1972.

J. V. Taylor, *The Christlike God*, London, SCM, 1992.

M. Taylor, *Not Angels but Agencies*, Geneva, WCC/SCM, 1995.

M. M. Thomas, *The Acknowledged Christ of the Indian Renaissance*, London, SCM, 1969.

J. Ward, *The Realm of Ends: Pluralism and Theism*, Cambridge, CUP, 1912.

T. Ware, *The Orthodox Church*, Harmondsworth, Penguin, 1973.

G. Warneck, *Protestant Missions*, Edinburgh, 1906.

H. Wheeler Robinson, *The Religious Ideas of the Old Testament*, London, Duckworth, 1913.

R. Williams, *Resurrection: Interpreting the Easter Gospel*, London, DLT, 1982.

W. Wink, *Engaging the Powers: Discernment and Resistance in a World of Domination*, Minneapolis, Fortress, 1992.

W. G. Young, *Patriarch, Shah and Caliph*, Rawalpindi, CSC, 1974.

R. C. Zaehner, *At Sundry Times*, London, Faber and Faber, 1958.

R. C. Zaehner, *Concordant Discord*, Oxford, OUP, 1970.

Notes

1 *Religious Faith in a Changing World*

1. A. Bunn, 'The Bohemian Girl II', in *The New Penguin Dictionary of Quotations* (Harmondsworth, Penguin, 1960).
2. See, for example, *The Other Side of 1984* (Geneva, WCC, 1983), pp. 5ff.; and *The Gospel in a Pluralist Society* (London, SPCK, 1989), pp. 14ff.
3. J. Hick, *God and the Universe of Faiths* (London, Collins, 1977), p. 131.
4. G. D'Costa, *Theology and Religious Pluralism* (Oxford, Blackwell, 1986), pp. 29f.
5. S. Radhakrishnan, *Indian Philosophy* (London, Allen and Unwin, 1923–7); *Eastern Religions and Western Thought* (Oxford, Clarendon Press, 1939).
6. H. Kraemer, *The Christian Message, in a Non-Christian World* (London, EHP, 1938); *Religion and the Christian Faith* (London, Lutterworth, 1956); W. Freytag, *The Gospel and the Religions* (London, SCM Press, 1957). For a recent discussion, see M. Barnes, *Religions in Conversation* (London, SPCK, 1989), pp. 34ff.
7. See, for example, K. Cragg, *Muhammad and the Christian: A Question of Response* (London, Darton, Longman and Todd, 1984), p. 13.
8. See, for example, G. Fackre, *Ecumenical Faith in Evangelical Perspective* (Grand Rapids, Eerdmans, 1993), pp. 89ff.; L. Newbigin, *The Other Side of 1984*, pp. 17ff.; *The Gospel in a Pluralist Society*, pp. 52ff.
9. See further, K. Cragg, *The Lively Credentials of God* (London, Darton, Longman and Todd, 1995), pp. 59ff.
10. L. Newbigin, *The Other Side of 1984*, p. 56.
11. C. F. D. Moule, *The Epistles to the Colossians and to Philemon* (Cambridge, Cambridge University Press, 1980), pp. 126ff.
12. See further, R. D. Sider, *The Gospel and its Proclamation: Message of the Fathers of the Church* (Delaware, Michael Glazier, 1983), pp. 40ff.
13. K. Cragg, *The Lively Credentials of God*, p. 239.
14. R. T. Wallis, *NeoPlatonism* (London, Duckworth, 1972).
15. See further, M. M. Thomas, *The Acknowledged Christ of the Hindu Renaissance* (London, SCM Press, 1969).
16. M. Iqbal, *The Development of Metaphysics in Persia* (Lahore, Bazm-i-Iqbal,

1954), p. 80; see also M. Nazir-Ali, *Islam: A Christian Perspective* (Exeter, Paternoster Press, 1983), pp. 61ff.

17. G. M. Hopkins, 'God's Grandeur', in *The New Oxford Book of English Verse* (Oxford, Oxford University Press, 1972), p. 786.

2 A Sense of the Sacred

1. K. Armstrong, *A History of God* (London, Heinemann, 1993), pp. 3ff.
2. J. V. Taylor, *The Primal Vision: Christian Presence and African Religion* (London, SCM Press, 1963); K. Bediako, *Christianity in Africa: The Renewal of a Non-Western Religion* (New York, Orbis, 1995).
3. J. S. Mbiti, *Introduction to African Religion* (Nairobi, Heinemann, 1991), pp. 45ff.
4. B. Idowu, *Olodumare – God in Yoruba Belief* (London, Longman, 1962), pp. 63ff.
5. See further, S. Neill, *A History of Christian Missions* (London, Penguin, 1990), pp. 138ff.
6. K. Bediako, *Christianity in Africa*, pp. 223ff.
7. J. S. Mbiti, *Introduction to African Religion*, p. 53.
8. K. Bediako, *Christianity in Africa*, pp. 216ff.
9. J. S. Mbiti, *Introduction to African Religion*, p. 45.
10. See further, R. K. Harrison, *Introduction to the Old Testament* (London, Tyndale Press, 1970), pp. 53ff.
11. See further, M. Nazir-Ali, *Frontiers in Muslim-Christian Encounter* (Oxford, Regnum Books, 1987), pp. 15f.; R. Bell, 'The Origin of Islam in its Christian Environment', *The Gunning Lectures* (London, Macmillan & Co., 1925), pp. 53f.
12. See, for example, his Oxford lecture, *Islam and the West* (Oxford Centre for Islamic Studies, 1993), pp. 19f.
13. K. Cragg, *The Lively Credentials of God* (London, Darton, Longman and Todd, 1995), pp. 76ff.
14. G. Von Rad, *Genesis* (London, SCM Press, 1972), p. 50. See also, *The Search for Faith and the Witness of the Church* (London, Church House Publishing, 1996), pp. 61ff.
15. See further, J. P. Hyatt, *Exodus* (Grand Rapids, Eerdmans, 1983), pp. 196ff.; A. D. H. Mayes, *Deuteronomy* (Grand Rapids, Eerdmans, 1979), pp. 64ff.; D. J. Wiseman, *I and II Kings* (Leicester, Inter-Varsity Press, 1993), pp. 97ff.
16. M. L. Snell, *Bernard Mizeki of Zimbabwe* (Gweru, Mambo Press, 1986).
17. K. Bediako, *Christianity in Africa*, p. 97.
18. See also, M. Nazir-Ali, *From Everywhere to Everywhere* (London, Collins, 1990), pp. 158ff.

19. L. Sanneh, *Translating the Message – The Missionary Impact on Culture* (New York, Orbis, 1989); K. Bediako, *Christianity in Africa*, pp. 109ff.

20. E. Sharpe, *The Goals of Inter-Religious Dialogue*, in J. Hick (ed.), *Truth and Dialogue* (London, Sheldon Press, 1974), pp. 77ff.; see also his *Not to Destroy but to Fulfil* (Uppsala, Gleerup, 1965).

21. Dom Bede Griffiths, *Christ in India* (New York, Springfield, Ill., Templegate, 1967), pp. 46ff.

22. G. Steiner, *Real Presences* (London, Faber and Faber, 1989), pp. 3ff., 137ff.

23. See also, M. Nazir-Ali, *Mission and Dialogue* (London, SPCK, 1995), pp. 117ff.

24. P. Davies, *The Mind of God* (London, Penguin, 1992), p. 90.

25. H. Montefiore, *The Probability of God* (London, SCM Press, 1985), p. 171.

26. J. Polkinghorne, *Science and Creation* (London, SPCK, 1988), pp. 19ff.

27. P. Davies, *The Mind of God*, pp. 91ff., 183ff., 188ff., *et al.*

28. See further, R. Dawkins, *The Blind Watchmaker* (London, Penguin, 1988); F. Crick, *The Astonishing Hypothesis: The Scientific Search for the Soul* (London, Touchstone, 1995).

29. R. Swinburne, *Is There a God?* (Oxford, Oxford University Press, 1996), pp. 62–3.

30. See *The Search for Faith*, pp. 132ff.

31. *The Search for Faith*, pp. 8, 229 *et al.*

32. J. Polkinghorne, *Science and Creation*, pp. 15ff.

33. L. Newbigin, *The Gospel in a Pluralist Society* (London, SPCK, 1989), pp. 60ff.

34. See also, M. Nazir-Ali, *Frontiers in Muslim-Christian Encounter*, pp. 20ff.

35. K. Cragg, 'Islamic Theology: Limits and Bridges', in D. M. McCurry (ed.), *The Gospel and Islam* (Monrovia, MARC, 1979), p. 198.

36. M. Iqbal, *Payam-i-Mashriq* (Lahore, Sheikh Ghulam Ali and Sons, 1969), p. 207.

3   In Diverse Manners

1. See J. S. Mbiti, *Introduction to African Religion* (Nairobi, Heinemann, 1991), pp. 68ff.

2. K. Bediako, *Christianity in Africa: The Renewal of a Non-Western Religion* (New York, Orbis, 1995), pp. 97ff., 210ff.

3. See further, R. Pannikar, *The Unknown Christ of Hinduism* (London, Darton, Longman and Todd, 1981), pp. 148ff.

4. K. Ward, in *Rational Theology and the Creativity of God* (New York, Pilgrim, 1982).

5. P. Davies, *The Mind of God* (London, Penguin, 1992), pp. 181ff.

6. A. A. Anderson, *Psalms*, NC BC, (Grand Rapids, Eerdmans, 1983), Vol. I, pp. 260ff.; Vol. II, p. 754.

7. C. K. Barrett, *The New Testament Background: Selected Documents* (London, SPCK, 1961), p. 184.

8. C. K. Barrett, *The New Testament Background: Selected Documents*, p. 184.

9. See further, K. Cragg, *The Mind of the Qu'rān* (London, Allen and Unwin, 1973), pp. 44, 70 et al.

10. *The Holy Qu'rān: Text, Translation and Commentary* (Leicester, Islamic Foundation), p. 2066.

11. M. Iqbal, *The Reconstruction of Religious Thought in Islam* (Lahore, Ashraf, 1971), pp. 48ff.

12. M. Iqbal, 'Bal-i-Jibrāil', in *Kulliyat-i-Iqbal* (Lahore, Sheikh Ghulam Ali, 1973), p. 28.

13. See further, M. Nazir-Ali, *Frontiers in Muslim-Christian Encounter* (Oxford, Regnum Books, 1987), pp. 130ff.

14. J. S. Mbiti, *Introduction to African Religion*, p. 68; K. Bediako, *Christianity in Africa*, pp. 91ff.

15. K. Bediako, 'Christian Tradition and the African God Revisited', in D. Gitari and P. Benson (eds.), *The Living God* (Nairobi, Uzima Press, 1986), pp. 77ff.

16. K. Bediako, *Christianity in Africa*, pp. 216ff.

17. *A Kenyan Service of Holy Communion* (Nairobi, Uzima Press, 1989), pp. 23, 33.

18. K. Bediako, *Christianity in Africa*, pp. 223ff.

19. *A Kenyan Service of Holy Communion*, p. 33.

20. See further, J. V. Taylor, *The Christlike God* (London, SCM Press, 1992), pp. 101ff.

21. J. V. Taylor, *The Go-Between God* (London, SCM Press, 1972), pp. 18f.

22. For an account of his conversion see his *Al Munqidh Min Al-Dalal* (What Delivers from Error), Damascus, 1934.

23. M. Smith, *Rabi'a the Mystic and her Fellow Saints in Islam* (Cambridge, Cambridge University Press, 1928); J. N. D. Anderson, *God's Law and God's Love, An Essay in Comparative Religion* (London, Collins, 1980).

24. M. Nazir-Ali, *From Everywhere to Everywhere* (London, Collins, 1990), pp. 152ff.

25. J. V. Taylor, *The Christlike God*, pp. 123, 133 et al.

26. W. Wordsworth, 'Intimations of Immortality', in *The New Oxford Book of English Verse* (Oxford, Oxford University Press, 1972), p. 508.

27. K. Cragg, *The Lively Credentials of God* (London, Darton, Longman and Todd, 1995), pp. 59ff.

4 *Christ Has Died: Redemptive Suffering*

1. P. M. Gregorios, W. H. Lazareth and N. A. Nissiotis (eds.), *Does Chalcedon Divide or Unite?* (Geneva, WCC, 1981), p. 62.

2. *The Coptic Liturgy of St Basil* (Melbourne, Coptic Orthodox Church, 1976, p. 15.

3. See further, W. G. Young, *Patriarch, Shah and Caliph* (Rawalpindi, CSC, 1974), pp. 78ff. and 197ff.

4. R. C. Zaehner, *At Sundry Times* (London, Faber and Faber, 1958); G. Basetti-Sani, *The Koran in the Light of Christ* (Chicago, Franciscan Herald Press, 1977), pp. 139ff.

5. The rubric has been an embarrassment to Catholic Anglicans and was introduced in 1552 without parliamentary approval. It was removed in 1559 but was reinstated in 1662 with some modifications.

6. See further, J. V. Taylor, *The Christlike God* (London, SCM Press, 1992), pp. 136ff.

7. See *The Mystery of Salvation*, A Report by the Doctrine Commission of the Church of England (London, Church House Publishing, 1995), pp. 112f.

8. *The Mystery of Salvation*, p. 113.

9. R. J. Bauckham, 'Theology of the Cross' in S. B. Ferguson and D. F. Wright (eds.), *The New Dictionary of Theology*, (Leicester, Inter-Varsity Press, 1988), pp. 181ff.

10. D. Nicholls, 'Addressing God as Ruler', *British Journal of Sociology*, Vol. 44, No. 1, March, 1993, pp. 125ff.; *God and Government* (Croydon, Jubilee, 1991); *Deity and Domination* (London, Routledge, 1989).

11. K. Kitamori, *Theology of the Pain of God* (London, SCM Press, 1966).

12. J. Moltmann, *The Crucified God* (London, SCM Press, 1974).

13. See, for example, J. Sobrino, *Christology at the Crossroads* (London, SCM Press, 1978).

14. W. H. Vanstone, *Love's Endeavour, Love's Expense* (London, Darton, Longman and Todd, 1977).

15. K. Cragg, *The Lively Credentials of God* (London, Darton, Longman and Todd, 1995), p. 169.

16. See *Salvation and the Church*, Anglican-Roman Catholic International Commission (London, CHP/CTS, 1987), p. 17.

17. Fynn, *Mister God, This is Anna* (London, Fount, Harper Collins, 1974), p. 41.

18. C. E. B. Cranfield, *The Gospel according to St Mark* (Cambridge, Cambridge University Press, 1966), p. 342.

19. See further, Q'urān 37:107.

20. See further, *Cur Deus Homo* in F. S. Schmitt's edition of Anselm's work, Vol. II (Edinburgh, Bonnae, 1946).

21. G. Aulen, *Christus Victor* (London, SPCK, 1950), p. 175.
22. ARCIC, *The Final Report: Eucharistic Doctrine* (London, CTS/SPCK, 1982), p. 14.
23. *Baptism, Eucharist and Ministry*, Faith and Order Paper 111 (Geneva, WCC, 1982), p. 6.
24. *Unitatis Redintegratio*, Para. 3ff.; *Ut Unum Sint* (Vatican, 1995), pp. 14ff.
25. C. Hill, 'The Decree on Ecumenism: An Anglican View', *One in Christ* (Bedford, Turvey Abbey, 1990).
26. See further, D. W. Bebbington, *Evangelicalism in Modern Britain* (London, Unwin, 1989), pp. 147, 203, 287, *et al.*
27. L. Boff, *Ecclesio-Genesis: The Base Communities Reinvent the Church* (London, Collins, 1986), pp. 61ff.
28. Acts 20.7 and Justin Martyr, *First Apology* 65–67, for early instances of a weekly celebration.
29. W. Bright, 'And now, O Father, Mindful of the Love', *English Hymnal* (Oxford University Press and Mowbrays, 1933).
30. L. Boff, *Ecclesio-Genesis*, pp. 70ff.
31. See further, D. M. Gitari, 'Evangelism and Culture' in V. Samuel and A. Hauser (eds.), *Proclaiming Christ in Christ's Way* (Oxford, Regnum Books, 1989), pp. 101ff.
32. L. Newbigin, *The Gospel in a Pluralist Society* (London, SPCK, 1989), pp. 198ff.
33. J. Stott, *Only One Way: The Message of Galatians* (Leicester, WP, 1980), p. 105.

5 Christ Is Risen: Life after Life?

1. See further, H. Wheeler Robinson, *The Religious Ideas of the Old Testament* (London, Duckworth, 1913), pp. 91ff.
2. H. Wheeler Robinson, *The Religious Ideas of the Old Testament*, p. 96.
3. H. Wheeler Robinson, *The Religious Ideas of the Old Testament*, pp. 97ff.
4. I. Said, *Sharh Bisharat Luqa* (Beirut, NLC, 1970), pp. 395ff.; cf. K. E. Bailey, *Poet and Peasant: A Literary-Cultural Approach to the Parables in Luke* (Grand Rapids, Eerdmans, 1983), pp. 158ff.; also D. J. Penman, *The Parables of Jesus* (Melbourne, AIO, 1985), pp. 28ff.
5. C. Gore (ed.), *Lux Mundi: A Series of Studies in the Religion of the Incarnation* (London, John Murray, 1889); also Gore's *Dissertation on the Incarnation* (London, John Murray, 1895).
6. R. Kipling, 'The Benefactors', *Verse* (London, A. P. Watt Ltd, 1940).
7. Cf. R. Williams, *Resurrection: Interpreting the Easter Gospel* (London, Darton, Longman and Todd, 1982).
8. F. F. Bruce, *I and II Corinthians* (Grand Rapids, Eerdmans, 1986), p. 139.

9. See further, J. W. Wenham, *Easter Enigma* (Exeter, Paternoster Press, 1984), p. 63.

10. R. D. Sider, *The Gospel and its Proclamation: Message of the Fathers of the Church* (Delaware, Michael Glazier, 1983), pp. 47ff.; see also J. W. Wenham, *Easter Enigma*, pp. 79ff.

11. W. Pannenberg, *Jesus – God and Man* (London, SCM Press, 1968), pp. 27ff.; J. Sobrino, *Christology at the Crossroads* (London, SCM Press, 1978), pp. 248ff.

12. See further, J. Ward, *The Realm of Ends: Pluralism and Theism* (Cambridge, Cambridge University Press, 1912), pp. 270ff.; G. E. M. Anscombe, *Causality and Determination* (Cambridge, Cambridge University Press, 1971), p. 26ff.

13. C. K. Barrett, *The Gospel According to St John* (London, SPCK, 1967), p. 64.

14. St Athanasius, *De Incarnatione* (Oxford, Mowbrays, 1982), pp. 56ff.

15. *Christ and Christianity in Persian Poetry* (Basingstoke, Sohrab Books, Nd), pp. 20–1.

6 *Christ Will Come Again: Salvation and Judgement*

1. E. W. Heaton, *The Book of Daniel: Introduction and Commentary* (London, SCM Press, 1956), (Torch Bible Commentary), pp. 47f., 66f., 96f.; see also R. A. Anderson, *Signs and Wonders* (ITC, Grand Rapids, Eerdmans, 1984), pp. 149f. for some of the difficulties regarding the view that Iranian religious ideas substantially influenced this book.

2. See further H. H. Rowley, *The Growth of the Old Testament* (London, Hutchinson, University Library, 1969), pp. 152ff.; B. W. Anderson, *The Living World of the Old Testament*, 2nd edn (London, Longmans, 1974), pp. 536ff.

3. C. K. Barrett, *The Gospel According to St John* (London, SPCK, 1967), pp. 56f.

4. See further, J. Moltmann, *Theology of Hope* (London, SCM Press, 1967), pp. 216ff.

5. See M. Nazir-Ali, *From Everywhere to Everywhere* (London, Collins, 1990), pp. 43f.

6. G. Every, SSM, *The Byzantine Patriarchate* (London, SPCK, 1947), pp. 19ff.

7. D. W. Bebbington, *Evangelicalism in Modern Britain* (London, Unwin, 1989), pp. 81ff.

8. For an account of the various challenges see J. Moltmann, *The Coming of God: Christian Eschatology* (London, SCM Press, 1996).

9. W. Pannenberg, *Jesus – God and Man* (London, SCM Press, 1968),

pp. 66ff.; J. Moltmann, *Theology of Hope*, pp. 139ff.; see also *The Coming of God* (London, SCM Press, 1996), pp. 69ff.

10. See further, J. Sobrino, *Christology at the Crossroads* (London, SCM Press, 1978), pp. 236ff.

11. P. Teilhard de Chardin, *Le Milieu Divin* (London, Collins, 1960); *The Phenomenon of Man* (London, Collins, 1959); *The Future of Man* (London, Collins, 1964).

12. F. Fukuyama 'The End of History', *The National Interest*, no. 16 (Summer 1989).

13. S. P. Huntington, *The Clash of Civilisations and the Remaking of World Order* (New York, Simon and Schuster, 1996).

14. H. Küng and others, *Christianity and the World Religions* (London, SCM Press, 1993), pp. 440f.

15. See further M. Nazir-Ali, *Islam: A Christian Perspective* (Exeter, Paternoster Press, 1983), pp. 70ff.

16. See further, R. C. Zaehner, *Concordant Discord* (Oxford, Oxford University Press, 1970), p. 87.

17. J. Moltmann, *The Coming of God*, p. 117.

18. For a careful consideration of this issue, see C. Westermann, *Isaiah 40–66*, (London, SCM Press, 1985), pp. 92f., 206f.

19. D. Bosch, *Transforming Mission* (New York, Orbis, 1991), pp. 5, 291ff.

20. J. A. Soggin, *The Prophet Amos* (London, SCM Press, 1987), p. 143.

21. *Mathnawi-i-Maanawi* (Cambridge University Press, 1925–1940), Book V: 3025ff.

22. But see further, D. L. Edwards and J. R. W. Stott, *Essentials* (London, Hodder and Stoughton, 1988); cf. J. Moltmann, *The Coming of God*, pp. 108f.

23. J. A. T. Robinson, *Wrestling with Romans* (London, SCM Press, 1979).

24. See further, M. Nazir-Ali, 'The Messianic Idea' in *Common Ground: The Journal of the CCJ*, No. 2, 1996, pp. 11f.

7   *The Ground of Our Meeting*

1. G. Von Rad, *Genesis* (London, SCM Press, 1972), pp. 49f., 77; cf. A. A. Anderson, *Psalms 1–72* (Grand Rapids, Eerdmans, 1983), pp. 262f.; see also Job 26.13; Psalm 104.30, etc.

2. R. D. Sider, *The Gospel and its Proclamation: Message of the Fathers of the Church* (Delaware, Michael Glazier, 1983), pp. 60ff.

3. See further, J. V. Taylor, *The Go-Between God* (London, SCM Press, 1972), pp. 26ff.

4. H. Wheeler Robinson, *The Religious Ideas of the Old Testament* (London, Duckworth, 1934), pp. 46ff.

5. It is, perhaps, worth noting that there is a reserve in the pre-exilic

prophets to speak directly of the Spirit. This may have been due to earlier abuse but it has quite disappeared in the exile and afterwards.

6. F. F. Bruce, *I and II Corinthians* (Grand Rapids, Eerdmans, 1980), pp. 120f.

7. J. V. Taylor, *The Go-Between God*, pp. 17ff., 179ff.; see also J. Ratzinger, 'Christ, Faith and the Challenge of Cultures', *Origins*, March, 1995, Vol. 24, No. 41, pp. 679ff.

8. G. Khodr, 'Christianity in a Pluralistic World – The Economy of the Holy Spirit' in C. G. Patelos (ed.), *The Orthodox Church in the Ecumenical Movement* (Geneva, WCC, 1978), pp. 297ff.

9. J. Moltmann, *The Trinity and the Kingdom of God* (London, SCM Press, 1981), pp. 182ff.

10. J. N. D. Anderson, *God's Law and God's Love: An Essay in Comparative Religion* (London, Collins, 1980).

11. K. Cracknell, *Towards a New Relationship* (London, Epworth, 1986), p. 64.

12. G. Khodr, 'Christianity in a Pluralistic World', p. 305.

13. J. V. Taylor, *The Go-Between God*, pp. 179ff.

14. G. Khodr, 'Christianity in a Pluralistic World', p. 306.

15. J. V. Taylor, *The Go-Between God*, p. 182.

16. M. Nazir-Ali, *Mission and Dialogue: Proclaiming the Gospel in Every Age* (London, SPCK, 1995), pp. 8ff.

17. J. V. Taylor, *The Go-Between God*, pp. 184.

18. See further, M. Smith, *Studies in Early Mysticism in the Near and Middle-East* (London, Sheldon Press, 1931); also, M. Iqbal, *The Development of Metaphysics in Persia* (Lahore, Bazm-i-Iqbal, 1964), pp. 76ff.

19. K. Rahner, *Christianity and the Non-Christian Religions, Theological Investigations* 5 (London, Darton, Longman and Todd, 1966), pp. 115–34; see also M. Barnes, *Religions in Conversation* (London, SPCK, 1989), pp. 52ff.

20. G. M. Hopkins, 'God's Grandeur', in *The New Oxford Book of English Verse* (Oxford, Oxford University Press, 1972) p. 786.

21. J. V. Taylor, *The Go-Between God*, p. 27.

22. F. F. Bruce, *I and II Corinthians*, p. 162.

23. F. Hahn, quoted in J. Moltmann, *The Trinity and the Kingdom of God*, p. 125.

24. St Basil the Great, *On the Holy Spirit* (New York, St Vladimir's Press, 1980), pp. 11f., 71ff. and *passim*.

25. F. Hahn, in J. Moltmann, *The Trinity and the Kingdom of God*, p. 125.

26. C. K. Barrett, *The Gospel According to St John* (London, SPCK, 1967), p. 77.

27. J. Moltmann, *The Trinity and the Kingdom of God*, pp. 126f.

28. See further, M. Nazir-Ali, *From Everywhere to Everywhere* (London, Collins, 1990), pp. 104f.

29. *Prayers and Meditations of St Anselm*, (Harmondsworth, Penguin, 1973), p. 153.

30. Julian of Norwich, *Revelations of Divine Love* (Harmondsworth, Penguin, 1966), Chapter 59.

31. K. Pillai, unpublished.

32. See further, M. Nazir-Ali, *From Everywhere to Everywhere*, p. 105.

33. See further, *The New Brown-Driver-Briggs-Gesenius, Hebrew and English Lexicon*, (Massachusetts, Hendrickson, 1979), p. 924; H. Wehr, *A Dictionary of Modern Written Arabic* (Wiesbaden, Harrassowitz, 1971), p. 365; Mar Aprem, *A Grammar Guide to Aramaic* (Trichur, Mar Nasai Press, 1981), p. 56.

34. A. C. Thisleton, 'Working with Feminist Theology: Criteria for Biblical Debate', unpublished paper 1995, quoting J. Barr, *The Semantics of Biblical Language* (Oxford, Oxford University Press, 1961).

35. C. K. Barrett, *The Gospel According to St John*, p. 77.

36. J. M. Soskice, 'Trinity and "the Feminine Other"', *New Blackfriars*, January, 1994.

37. E. and J. Moltmann, *Humanity in God* (London, SCM Press, 1983), p. 103.

38. E. S. Fiorenza, *In Memory of Her: A Feminist Theological Reconstruction of Christian Origins* (London, SCM Press, 1983), pp. 184ff.

39. J. D. G. Dunn, *Unity and Diversity in the New Testament* (London, SCM Press, 1990), pp. 176ff.

40. See further, I. H. Marshall, *Acts* (Grand Rapids, Eerdmans, 1980), pp. 69f.; W. R. Davies, 'Glossolalia' in G. S. Wakefield (ed.), *A Dictionary of Christian Spirituality* (London, SCM Press, 1983).

41. F. F. Bruce, *I and II Corinthians* (Grand Rapids, Eerdmans, 1971), pp. 117f.

42. J. D. G. Dunn, *Unity and Diversity in the New Testament*, pp. 174ff.

43. D. W. Bebbington, *Evangelicalism in Modern Britain* (London, Unwin, 1989), p. 229ff.

44. A. Richards, *The Toronto Experience: An Exploration of the Issues* (London, CHP, 1997), pp. 3f., S. Jebb, *No Laughing Matter* (Bromley, Day One, 1995), pp. 15f.

45. A. Richards, *The Toronto Experience*, p. 4; W. J. Hollenweger, *The Pentecostals* (London, SCM Press, 1972).

46. S. Jebb, *No Laughing Matter*, pp. 13, 25.

47. G. Carey, *The Gate of Glory* (London, Hodder and Stoughton, 1992), p. 202.

48. W. J. Hollenweger, *The Pentecostals*, pp. 75ff.; see also V. Samuel and C. M. N. Sugden (eds.), *Sharing Jesus in the Two-Thirds World* (Bangalore, PIM, 1983).

49. J. S. Mbiti, *Introduction to African Religion* (Oxford, Heinemann, 1975), pp. 54ff.

50. M. L. Snell, *Bernard Mizeki of Zimbabwe* (Gweru, Mambo Press, 1986), p. 17.

8 *What Is Man (or Woman)?*

1. See further, J. Hick, *Evil and the God of Love* (Basingstoke, Macmillan, 1985), p. 211.
2. P. Davies, *The Mind of God: Scientific Basis for a Rational World* (London, Penguin, 1993), pp. 22ff.
3. Roman Liturgy for Holy Saturday, *The New Marian Missal* (Bombay, Paulist Press, 1961).
4. *Apologia Pro Vita Sua* (London, Collins, 1959), p. 278; cf. Ephesians 2:12.
5. A. Tennyson, 'Ulysses', in *The New Oxford Book of English Verse* (Oxford, Oxford University Press, 1972), p. 646.

9 *Embassy, Hospitality and Dialogue: Christians and People of Other Faiths*

1. See further, J. Stambaugh and D. Balch, *The Social World of the First Christians* (London, SPCK, 1986), pp. 41ff., 127ff.; W. G. Young, *Patriarch, Shah and Caliph* (Rawalpindi, CSC, 1974), pp. 3ff.
2. R. Bell, *The Origin of Islam in its Christian Environment* (London, Frank Cass, 1926); and M. Nazir-Ali, *Islam: A Christian Perspective* (Exeter, Paternoster Press, 1983).
3. A. Mar Thoma, *The Mar Thoma Church: Heritage and Mission* (Tiruvalla, Ashram Press, 1985).
4. R. D. Sider, *The Gospel and its Proclamation: Message of the Fathers of the Church* (Delaware, Michael Glazier, 1983).
5. W. G. Young, *Patriarch, Shah and Caliph*, pp. 15f.
6. D. J. Sahas, *John of Damascus on Islam* (Leiden, Brill, 1972); M. S. Seale, *Muslim Theology* (London, Luzac & Co., 1964); and M. Nazir-Ali, *Frontiers in Muslim-Christian Encounter* (Oxford, Regnum Books, 1987), pp. 17f., 49.
7. See further, M. T. Clark (ed.), *An Aquinas Reader* (London, Hodder and Stoughton, 1972), pp. 15ff.
8. In *Encounters and Clashes* (Rome, Pontifical Institute for the Study of Arabic and Islamics, 1984), pp. 161.
9. G. Warneck, *Protestant Missions* (Edinburgh, Oliphant, 1906); D. Bosch, *Transforming Mission* (New York, Orbis, 1992), pp. 239ff; M. Nazir-Ali, *From Everywhere to Everywhere* (London, Collins, 1990), pp. 42ff.
10. See, for instance, S. Neill, *A History of Christian Missions* (London, Penguin, 1986), pp. 156ff.
11. See further, J. N. Farquhar, *The Crown of Hinduism* (Oxford, Oxford

University Press, 1913). See also M. Barnes, *Religions in Conversation* (London, SPCK, 1989).

12. A. Atiya, *Eastern Christianity* (London, Methuen, 1968); H. Hill (ed.), *Light from the East* (Toronto, Anglican Book Centre, 1988).

13. See, for example, J. C. England (ed.), *Living Theology in Asia* (London, SCM Press, 1981), pp. 191ff.

14. A. Powell, *Muslims and Missionaries in Pre-Mutiny India* (Richmond, Surrey, Curzon Press, 1993).

15. H. Küng (ed.), *Christianity and the World Religions* (London, SCM Press, 1986).

16. *Nostra Aetate*, A. Flannery (ed.), *Documents of Vatican II* (New York, Costello, 1987), pp. 738ff.; cf. M. Barnes, *Religions in Conversation*, pp. 50f.

17. *Guidelines on Religious Relations with the Jews* (CRRJ, 1974).

18. R. Coleman (ed.), *Resolutions of the Twelve Lambeth Conferences* (Toronto, Anglican Book Centre, 1992).

19. See further, *The Truth Shall Make You Free: the Lambeth Conference, 1988* (London, ACC, 1988), Resolutions 20 and 21 and Appendix 6; The World Council of Churches, *Guidelines on Dialogue* (Geneva, WCC, 1979); Council of Churches for Britain and Ireland, *Christian Identity – Witness and Interfaith Dialogue* (London, CCBI, 1991).

20. *Adisthan: Sacred Space* (Bangalore, NBCLC, 1993); see also *Communities and Buildings*, a Report of the Church of England's Inter-Faith Consultative Group, (London, Church House Publishing, 1996).

21. M. M. Thomas, *The Acknowledged Christ of the Indian Renaissance* (London, SCM Press, 1969).

22. K. Cragg, *To Meet and to Greet* (London, Epworth, 1992); cf. C. Lamb, *A Call to Retrieval* (London, Grey Seal, 1997).

23. See M. Nazir-Ali, *Islam: A Christian Perspective* (Exeter, Paternoster Press, 1983), pp. 37, 86.

24. See A. Mar Thoma, *The Mar Thoma Church: Heritage and Mission*, pp. 2f.

25. See further, *Communities and Buildings*.

26. In D. Cohn-Sherbok (ed.), *Many Mansions: Interfaith and Religious Intolerance* (London, Canterbury Press, 1992), pp. 149ff.

27. See further, *Multi-faith Worship?* from the Interfaith Consultative Group (London, Church House Publishing, 1992).

28. J. A. Beckford and S. Gilliat, *The Church of England and Other Faiths in a Multi-Faith Society* (Coventry, University of Warwick, 1996).

29. See further, R. Hooker and C. Lamb, *Love the Stranger: Ministry in Multi-Faith Areas* (London, SPCK, 1993).

30. *Christian Identity, Witness and Interfaith Dialogue*, pp. 5f.

31. J. A. T. Robinson, *Truth is Two-Eyed* (London, SCM Press, 1979), p. 129 (quoting Sloane Coffin).

32. J. Goldingay, *Theological Diversity and the Authority of the Old Testament* (Grand Rapids, Eerdmans, 1987).

33. See further, W. Brueggemann, 'Trajectories in Old Testament Literature and the Sociology of Ancient Israel', *Journal of Biblical Literature*, 1979, No. 98, pp. 161–85; also M. H. Woudstra, *The Book of Joshua* (Grand Rapids, Eerdmans, 1981), pp. 37f.

34. See G. Von Rad, *Genesis* (London, SCM Press, 1972), pp. 179f.

35. See further, J. A. Soggin, *The Prophet Amos* (London, SCM Press, 1987), pp. 142.

36. For an extended discussion, see J. G. Baldwin, *Haggai, Zechariah and Malachi* (London, Tyndale Pess, 1972), pp. 227ff.

37. O. Kaiser, *Isaiah 13–39* (London, SCM Press, 1974), pp. 111.

38. J. Stambaugh and D. Balch, *The Social World of the First Christians*, pp. 54ff.

39. J. V. Taylor, *The Go-Between God* (London, SCM Press, 1972), pp. 42f., 127f.

40. G. Khodr, 'Christianity in a Pluralistic World – The Economy of the Holy Spirit' in C. G. Patelos (ed.), *The Orthodox Church in the Ecumenical Movement* (Geneva, WCC, 1978), pp. 297ff.

41. *Dialogue and Proclamation*, Pontifical Council for Inter-Religious Dialogue, Rome, *The Bulletin*, May 1991; E. J. Sharpe, 'The Goals of Inter-Religious Dialogue', in J. Hick (ed.), *Truth and Dialogue* (London, SPCK, 1974), pp. 77ff.

42. H. Küng (ed.), *Christianity and the World Religions* (London, SCM, 1993), pp. 44off.; also his Lambeth Interfaith Lecture, *World Politics and World Ethics as a Challenge to the Churches*, November, 1994.

43. Geneva, WCC, 1979, pp. 11. Such thinking is widespread in ecumenical documents and has, more recently, been reaffirmed by the Committee for Relations with People of Other Faiths of the Council of Churches for Britain and Ireland in *Christian Identity, Witness and Interfaith Dialogue*.

44. M. Percy, *Words, Wonders and Power* (London, SPCK, 1996), pp. 9ff.

45. M. Nazir-Ali, *Mission and Dialogue* (London, SPCK, 1995), pp. 85.

46. E.g. R. J. Rushdoony, *The Institutes of Biblical Law* (Phillipsburg NJ, Presbyterian and Reformed, 1973). For a critique, see G. R. Fackre, *Ecumenical Faith in Evangelical Perspective* (Grand Rapids, Eerdmans, 1993).

10   Religion and Conflict in the World Today

1. S. P. Huntington, *The Clash of Civilisations and the Remaking of World Order* (New York, Simon& Schuster, 1996), pp. 40ff.

2. See further, T. Ware, *The Orthodox Church* (Harmondsworth, Penguin, 1973), pp. 82ff.; H. Hill (ed.), *Light from the East: A Symposium on the*

Oriental Orthodox and Assyrian Churches (Toronto, Anglican Book Centre, 1988), pp. 14ff.

3. S. P. Huntington, *The Clash of Civilisations and the Remaking of World Order*, pp. 301ff.

4. See further, M. Nazir-Ali, *Islam: A Christian Perspective* (Exeter, Paternoster Press, 1983), pp. 102ff.

5. See further, V. S. Naipaul, *India: A Million Mutinies Now* (London, Heinemann, 1990).

6. See further, M. Nazir-Ali, *Mission and Dialogue* (London, SPCK, 1995), pp. 84ff.

7. F. F. Gibson, *The Gospel According to St Matthew* (London, A & C Black, 1971), p. 78.

8. But see further, W. Wink, *Engaging the Powers: Discernment and Resistance in a World of Domination* (Minneapolis, Fortress, 1992), pp. 209ff.

9. M. T. Ahmad, *Murder in the Name of Allah* (Cambridge, Lutterworth Press, 1989).

10. A. Y. Ali, *The Holy Qu'rān: Text, Translation and Commentary* (Leicester, The Islamic Foundation, 1975), p. 103.

11. R. Thamotheram, *South Africa's Transition and its Implications for Countries experiencing Civil Conflict*, 1995, p. 6f.

12. S. P. Huntington, *The Clash of Civilisations and the Remaking of World Order*, pp. 316ff.

13. See further, K. Cragg, *Muhammad and the Christian: A Question of Response* (London, Darton, Longman and Todd, 1984); *Jesus and the Muslim: An Exploration* (London, Unwin, 1985).

14. S. P. Huntington, *The Clash of Civilisations and the Remaking of World Order*, pp. 318ff.

15. H. Küng, *Christianity and the World Religions* (London, SCM Press, 1993).

11   Jubilee: a Theme for the Millennium

1. See further, M. Nazir-Ali, *Mission and Dialogue* (London, SPCK, 1995), pp. 37ff.

2. I. Linden, *Mission and Liberation in the New World Disorder* (London, USPG, 1997).

3. See further, *Unemployment and the Future of Work: An Enquiry for the Churches* (London, CCBI, 1997).

4. See further, R. K. Harrison, *Leviticus: An Introduction and Commentary* (Leicester, IVP, 1980), pp. 223ff.; J. Goldingay, *Theological Diversity and the Authority of the Old Testament* (Grand Rapids, Eerdmans, 1987), pp. 59ff.; J. A. Thompson, 'Tirzah' in *The Illustrated Bible Dictionary* (Sydney, Hodder and Stoughton, 1980), pp. 1571f.

5. Trinity Communications, Manassas, VA, 1994, pp. 5ff.

6. P. Selby, *Grace and Mortgage* (London, Darton, Longman and Todd, 1997), pp. xiii, 30ff., 73ff.
7. See further, M. Taylor, *Not Angels but Agencies* (London/Geneva, WCC/SCM, 1995), pp. 2, 137ff.
8. See further, *This Menace of Bonded Labour* (London, Anti-Slavery International, 1996).

12 *Towards a Spiritual and Moral Framework for Society*

1. See further, J. Habgood, *Finding A Moral Heart for Europe*, Windsor Lecture, St George's House, Windsor, 1992.
2. D. Berher and others, *European Values Study, 1981–1990* (London, David Cook Foundation, 1992); see also *The Search for Faith and Witness of the Church* (London, Church House Publishing, 1996), pp. 1ff.
3. See further, T. Modood (ed.), *Church, State and Religious Minorities* (London, Policy Studies Inst., 1997).

13 *A Ministry of Reconciliation*

1. G. A. Studdert Kennedy, Easter Hymn, *The Unutterable Beauty* (London, Hodder & Stoughton, 1970), p. 92.

Index of Names and Subjects

INDEX OF NAMES AND SUBJECTS

Index of Biblical References

195

Index of Qu'rānic References